Abused • Addicted • Free

The inspiring true story of Trudy Makepeace

Trudy Makepeace

First published 2021 by Sarah Grace Publishing
an imprint of Malcolm Down Publishing Ltd.
www.sarahgracepublishing.co.uk

24 23 22 21 7 6 5 4 3 2 1

British Library Cataloguing in Publication Data
A catalogue record for this book is available from the British Library.

ISBN 978-1-912863-81-5

Cover design by Esther Kotecha
Art direction by Sarah Grace
Cover Artist Emma Holloway

Printed in the UK

Endorsements

For the past 25 years I have had the privilege of being able to minister and walk alongside men and women who suffer from addiction. In the course of those years, I have witnessed the Lord perform many miracles in lives that were once ravaged and bound by addiction, now transformed through the power of His gospel.

This book conveys Trudy's personal story and I truly commend her for her courage and desire to share it. Yet, it is not just her story that is remarkable, but also God's story; a story that clearly expresses His heart. Here is the God who never gives up on us and devises ways so that a 'banished person may not remain estranged from Him' (2 Samuel 14:14).

I was moved to tears many times reading of how God touched Trudy's heart and would not give up on her even when she had given up on herself and eventually how His unfailing love won her over and set her free to be the beautiful woman she is today.

This book will not only encourage those lost in addiction that there is a way out, but will also inspire outreach workers, rehabilitation workers and churches who open their doors and hearts to those who are bound in addiction. The message is DON'T GIVE UP, because no one is a lost cause in God's eyes!

Along with the many success stories there are also disappointments, but Trudy's story shows us that once God touches a life, they are never the same again. Our role in His amazing plan is to continue being obedient in bringing this wonderful Gospel of Jesus Christ, the Gospel of HOPE to the hopeless and allow God to do the rest as He did with Trudy. The reader of this book will be touched and inspired!

Fiona Fallon

National Programme Director, Teen Challenge UK

Few autobiographies I have read have been written with such transparent honesty as this powerful book from Trudy Makepeace. In the same way that a jeweller displays a diamond against a dark background to enhance its beauty, so the author portrays her story against the harshest contexts of abuse and exploitation. Yet what the author asks us to focus on is not her triumph over harrowing adversity, but rather she directs us to the grace of God and the victory He gives to all who will put their lives in His hands. I fully recommend this book.

John Glass

Elim General Superintendent 2000-2016 and Chair of Council, Evangelical Alliance 2014-2018

I first met Trudy eleven years ago through a mutual friend when she was with a group of young ladies from the rehabilitation home that she led. She is one of the most selfless and loving people I have ever met, a champion for the broken destitute and marginalized. Her story is living proof that miracles still happen today. Trudy is an anointed and gifted evangelist and minister of the Gospel. It is my privilege to be her friend. I am sure that many lives will be moved by her compelling true-life story.

Rev. Marilyn Harry

Elim Minister (retired), Evangelist Love Wales

Trudy's story is a story many can identify with, but it's so much more. Every page reveals two consistent realities: the brokenness of the human heart and the beauty of God. Written with breath-taking self-awareness, you are drawn into the most terrifying of realities that without God humanity has little hope. Trudy is a living miracle, marked by the mercy of God and filled with unquenchable passion to live her life for Jesus. This book will change many lives because it exposes a profound truth in every heart: that we are all looking for the right thing but in all the wrong places.

Rev Simon Foster

Elim Minister, Elim National Leadership Team 2008-2018

Trudy's story is a powerful witness to the life-giving power of the Gospel of Jesus Christ. It is a reminder to anyone that no matter how hard life has hit you, Christ's love can heal and restore. At Trudy's home church, we get the privilege of seeing the story continue through her ministry to the street homeless in Bristol. God's relentless grace fills the pages of this book and I know it will be a source of hope for anyone who picks it up.

Rev. Stephen McEwen

Senior Leader of E5 Church Bristol

Through the unveiling of her own life, Trudy tells of seedy underworlds that exist all around us. Trudy found freedom, but many are still trapped. I cried and felt Trudy's pain as I read the book; you will too. Gripped by every page, I was reminded of the true hope that only God can give. A hope that goes beyond all barriers, to all depths and around all things to unleash people's true potential. Trudy is a shining example of that reality.

Clyde Thomas

Director of Hope Centre Ministries & Lead Minister at Victory Church

What a story! Trudy's journey shows that there is always hope, even when the odds are against you from the off. I totally endorse this book. Buy it, then fasten your seat belt!

Barry Woodward

Author of *Once an Addict* & Director of Proclaim Trust

Trudy has held nothing back in these pages, which so beautifully and at times brutally identify key moments of her transformation. It is an honour to know Trudy and bear witness to her passion and love for people and God. Trudy has shown it's possible to dance with no music; she is a true disciple of hope.

Helen Yousaf
Worship Leader, Elim Minister

Dedication

I would like to dedicate this book to those who are yet to find hope, healing and freedom from addiction, shame, abuse and trauma, and other life controlling issues.

Contents

Prologue: Broken

"Shut up!" he shouted in a Brummie accent. "Turn round!" He grabbed my throat with one hand and pushed the edge of a blade to my neck with the other. "One wrong move and I'll cut your throat!"

I felt the cold edge of the knife against my flesh. I shivered as he pushed the tip deeper into my skin.

"Who do you think you are?" he shouted. Fear gripped my heart as he traced the blade across my throat; it could all be over in seconds. "Turn around now."

As I turned, he punched me in the back of the head. Shockwaves reeled through my body. I had no time to think as he threw another punch, this time to the side of my head. I pressed my face into the seat to protect myself. My head was throbbing. He grabbed my neck and shoved my face down harder into the car seat and started to beat my side and back. His hands were big and his knuckles strong.

I was at his mercy. He was bigger than me and it would take little for the blade to slip. Then it would all be over. I closed my eyes and stopped resisting. If I wanted to get out of the car alive, the only thing to do was submit.

"Alright, whatever you want, okay?" I cried out.

Having turned around, I was now face down on the car seat and he was raping me. As he ruthlessly pounded himself into me, I vowed I was not going to leave empty-handed. I had already slyly slipped a fifty pound note out of his back pocket. I'd tucked it into my black leather boot when he had pushed me down on his lap. I was already planning how and where I would score my drugs. I knew it was a gamble – at any minute he could have slit my throat – but I was fixated on getting high whatever the cost. I knew the risk, but I felt my way back round to the back of his jeans and slid the two tips of my fingers into the top of his pocket. Another note! My heart was racing, but his focus was elsewhere. *Come on Trudy, just grab it.* I pulled the money out. All I had to do was get the note into my boot, but I was pinned down and unable to move. I crumpled it up as small as possible and gripped it in the palm of my hand. *Don't aggravate him. Just stay alive.*

He finished with a grunt. The heavy weight of his body lifted as he pulled himself off me, his dreadlocks irritating me as they brushed the side of my neck and face. I opened my clutched hand, saw the twenty-pound note and slipped it into my boot. *I've got to get out of here. God, please do not let him check his trousers.*

He started the car. I had no idea where we were heading.

Suddenly, he started to whimper.

"I'm so sorry."

He had morphed into a remorseful child. I couldn't believe it. This man was three times my size. He had just beaten and raped me. But now he was apologetic and pathetic, expecting me to forgive him. For one crazy second, I almost felt sorry for him. I turned my face to stare out the window.

It was still dark, and he pulled into an industrial estate. He stopped the car, leant over me and opened the door. Still apologising, he pushed me out onto the pavement. As I fell, the heel on my boot snapped. I was lost and alone. I stared at my boot — *broken.*

As I saw the back of his black car moving away, I dragged myself up from the road and crawled to the curb. Holding my head in my hands, I began to sob. I staggered through the streets in pain and made it back to the hostel where my partner Jake was waiting for me.

Standing in front of the mirror, I saw my gaunt pale image and sunken lifeless eyes looking back at me. Suddenly I saw how broken I was and that this hopeless mess had become normal. I collapsed on the bed, seeking some solace and comfort to soothe my aching body and my tormented heart. For three days, my whole body ached. I was in shock. I had become accustomed to abuse, violence and pain. I already knew what it was to be discarded, rejected and abandoned. But now I felt defeated.

I had no idea then that one day all these fragmented pieces would become a beautiful mosaic, revealing a different picture from the distorted, fractured one I could see that night.

Chapter 1: Silenced

I was just four when those fateful words flew out of my mouth.

"I've got two mums!"

"What did you say?" Mum yelled. She dealt me a swift backhander sending me hurtling to the floor. Shocked, I grabbed my ear that was now ringing and throbbing and stared at her. "Don't ever say that again, do you hear me?" I could see she was furious.

Everything in me seized up; I lay there stunned, holding onto my sore ear. *Why did she hit me? What did I do?* Fear and silence gripped me. In that moment, I learned it was not safe to speak out.

When she was just seventeen, my biological mum Eileen ran away from home to join a hippy convoy in Nottingham for a few months, and when she returned, she was pregnant. Premature, unplanned and unwanted, my entrance into the world was a huge shock to her and the whole family. When I was six months old, Eileen agreed to allow her older brother Malcolm and his wife Tina to adopt me. What really went on has always depended on which member of the family you listen to.

I was officially adopted by the age of two in 1975. My name changed from Seward to Makepeace. Tina, my adopted mum, often took us to grandad Seward when we went into the town centre of Newbury, the little market town where we lived. Eileen still lived with Grandad on the edge of town in a row of cottages built after the war. The family moved there in the 1950s after leaving their previous home, condemned due to part of the roof missing.

As a child, I enjoyed our weekly visits to Grandad's; there was something comforting about visiting him. Grandad was a short but robust man. He still had a bit of thinning hair and a glorious bald patch that shimmered with sweat, and he walked with a bit of a limp. I often wondered as I listened to his old war stories if his limp was because of a war injury, or if it was just that he was born with one leg shorter than the other. He was always dressed in his old plain work shirt unbuttoned to his chest with sleeves firmly rolled up; Grandad was and had always been a real grafter.

During one of our visits, when I was just four, Grandad was sitting in his tall upright chair, which apparently helped rest his leg as he watched the news broadcast. The room was dimly lit and smoke fumes filled the air. Grandad rolled his tobacco, licking the rizla before reaching for the lighter.

"Bloody government, they can't get anything right," he muttered to himself. "I've worked my whole life and now they want to take even more money from us, it's a damn right disgrace."

I ran over to where he sat. My eye caught the antique wooden coffee table beneath the TV, which was laden with pornographic magazines and a magnifying glass. I tried to ignore them; the pictures made me feel uncomfortable. I turned my eyes instead to the news presenter on the TV.

Later that afternoon I was being my usual inquisitive self and chased Grandad into the kitchen to see what he was up to. He was limping slightly as he made his way towards the fridge, pulling out his regular spam lunch. My two aunties, Eileen and Jane, were talking, although as the stronger character of the two, Auntie Jane was the one doing most of the talking. Jane was Eileen's older sister.

"She has a right to know!" she insisted, nagging Eileen and looking for Grandad to give her his moral support. Looking me straight in the eye, she blurted out, "Somebody needs to tell her!"

Tell her what? I wondered.

"Your mum's not your real mum, your Auntie Eileen is."

I stared back at her, dumbfounded. I looked at Eileen, then Grandad. The room went silent.

Eileen's my mum?

I was in shock. Her words seemed to vibrate through my entire brain and body as my tiny mind struggled to take in this new information. I looked over at Auntie Eileen. Up to this point, all I knew about her was that she liked to smoke, drink coke and eat pies. She also loved to laugh a lot and was always kind to me. *I've got two mums!*

I attempted to consider the added benefits, unsure of what they were, and for a split second I thought, *I must be special to have two mums!* Bursting at the seams with newfound joy, I was eager to share my good news. Excited, I ran into the front room where Tina, my adopted mum, was sitting next to the fireplace in the old dusty armchair. Unable to contain the news and with a proud smile on my face, the words came hurtling out.

"I've got two mums!"

Then came that backhander that silenced me.

Saddened and bewildered by the events, I played the same old record in my head again and again. *There must be something wrong with me. I am the problem. I don't belong here.* From that time on, Tina avoided talking about the subject of the adoption, and I knew better than to ask. Now silenced from asking about my identity, shame came and overshadowed me. That shame came to point the finger and tell me there was something wrong with me.

Over the years, I pieced together bits of my adopted mum's history. Tina had grown up one of five children. Her dad was in the RAF and her family eventually settled in South Wales. At eighteen, she married Malcolm to escape life at home. Malcolm had always lived with Grandad, although he had a different father to Eileen and her younger brother. Nan and Grandad separated and the family split. Auntie Jane went to live with Nan and Malcolm, and Eileen's younger brother had been left with Grandad. So, when Tina and Malcolm got married, they lived at his house. For some reason, they were not able to conceive. It was during this time Eileen discovered she was pregnant.

The only time I ever recall Tina talking about the adoption was when I was five or six; we were walking back home from one of our regular visits to Grandad's. There had been a conversation where Grandad asked if my mum had spoken to me about the events. I hurriedly walked to keep up with her as she pushed the pram on our way home.

"Eileen could not cope with having a baby, that's why we adopted you," she said suddenly, in her authoritative tone. "It's as simple as that! She was in no fit state to look after you. She would not change your nappy and left you crying when you needed feeding. I was the one who looked after you, I was the one who wanted you, and that's the end of the matter."

Mum's desire for a child had been no secret; she had maintained she was unable to have her own children. Ironically, she went on to have four of her own after adopting me. It was later in my teens that I discovered some of those in the family sided with Eileen and been of the opinion that 'some people' had taken advantage of her and the situation.

Later, at the age of fourteen when I was in the care of social services, I worked after school with Eileen doing some cleaning jobs. Gradually parts of the story came out as we spent time together. I began to ask questions. I wanted to know why there had been such secrecy and what actually happened. Eileen was big in size and heart and oozed warmth and sensitivity. Over time, she began to open up to me, something I knew she did not find easy. On one occasion, as we headed to the offices, she stopped in her tracks and spoke as though she was revealing something she had waited a long time to tell me.

"I didn't want to give you up," she said, tears welling up in her eyes. I didn't like to see her in pain.

"It's okay, I understand," I said, but my understanding was limited. I had always known she was not in the best circumstances to take care of me, and I had learned to accept it. What's more, Mum's backhander had taught me that it was not safe to ask questions, but just to accept things the way they were.

But deep down, I still had unresolved questions. I needed answers. I wanted to know who I really was, and who my father was.

Later the following week, as we stepped into the offices to clean, I came back to the previous conversation that seemed to have been cut short.

"Eileen, last week you said you did not want to give me up, so why did you?" I asked tentatively.

"I had no money, no job, I was on my own. I never had planned to get pregnant." She paused. "It was a lot to cope with, a newborn baby. It got even harder when I heard the news that Howard, your dad, died of a brain tumour when you were just six months old. It was a really difficult and emotional time."

She sat down on the chair and I sat beside her, grabbing hold of every word in this precious moment I was able to steal with her.

"Your 'mum' had just taken over and, at the time, it was easy to let her. As time went on, I felt under more and more pressure to let Malcolm and Tina take you. They could offer you a better life."

I felt her inner turmoil and her obvious sincerity as she spoke. The pain and regret locked up inside of her was palpable.

"Sorry Trudy, by the time I realised I had made a mistake and wanted to keep you, it was too late." Regret, sorrow, suppressed emotion and powerlessness resonated in her voice. She bowed her head and looked away. "When your dad found out your mum was pregnant with your sister Sarah, he took me aside into the garden up at Hill Close, and he offered to sell you back to me for two hundred pounds… Where was I going to get two hundred pounds? I didn't have that kind of money. Now Tina was pregnant, they didn't want you. I knew I had made a mistake, but it was too late."

It went silent. My heart sank. I loved my dad; he was the one I thought I could count on. I was gutted, I felt betrayed.

My biological father, on the other hand, has always been a mystery. His name is not on my birth certificate. Apparently, no one in the family met him – he was Eileen's best kept secret. Growing up, I had loads of questions and doubts. Did Eileen even know who my dad was? I was never sure if she just spun me a yarn or told the truth. Eileen said my father died of a brain tumour, the result of a motorbike accident when I was six months old, but that he had met me as a baby. It was hard for me to accept what she said, because I was never able to trace him. The hiddenness of her secret covered the shame she felt, possibly of who he was and what had happened.

I never really did find out and now all three have passed away. I still wonder what really happened to Eileen all those years ago.

Chapter 2: Shamed

My life really started to freefall at the age of five. The events which began at that time inevitably shaped the person I would become.

My mum and dad were going out for the evening. John, who was close to the family, was babysitting. I looked up from the floor where I sat as my mum flicked her long, thick jet-black hair from beneath the collar of her coat before doing up her buttons. It was a rare occasion for them to go out together in those days.

"Right, straight to bed at seven thirty, young lady," Dad insisted.

"Make sure that Trudy has her camomile lotion on before she goes up," Mum added to John.

My two younger sisters had already been put to bed. I sat watching the start of a gameshow on our old portable black and white TV. Despite the coat hanger that served as our aerial, the picture would cut out at the best bits. Still, I was captivated as I watched the dancers whirl around the stage. I loved their glittering outfits and the way they moved their bodies in sync with such energy and precision. I imagined what life would be like as a dancer. As the routine drew to a close, I knew it was my cue for bed, but I felt uneasy. Something didn't feel quite right. John called me over and made me stand a few feet away from where he sat.

"Come on, take off your nightie, it's time for your lotion."

I did what I was told. Standing in my pants, his look made me feel naked, awkward and embarrassed. I felt violated even at that age. Alone and helpless, my eyes fell to the brown bottle that was propped next to him on the arm of the old worn orange chair he was sitting in.

"Come closer."

I wanted to run, but I was overpowered by fear. I went closer. Something in my throat was almost choking me as he started with the lotion and took me to the sofa. Fragments of that night are still etched in my memory; him on top of me and me barely able to breathe with his hands all over me.

The following day I was desperate to tell someone, but a voice echoed in my mind. *No one cares, no one will listen to you. You'll just get walloped again.*

As the time continued to pass, it became harder to pluck up the courage to find the words to tell my mum what had happened. We had just had our 50p electric meter robbed. I remember sitting on the doorstep, trying to decide whether to tell my mum about what happened.

There's no point. They won't believe you. Mum is more worried about the electric meter.

Of course, she had no idea, but I felt unimportant and insignificant. I sat wishing she would notice me out there, hoping that she would realise that something was wrong. I wanted to tell, but it became my shameful secret.

For the days and months following, I walked around in a daze, confused and disorientated. I had a new constant companion; a dark looming shadow that followed me everywhere. I found escapism in daydreaming and shutting down emotionally. I couldn't process what was going on inside me; I thought that by not thinking or talking about it the sadness would go. But instead, it became buried deeper inside. I wanted to run, to run away from myself, from my shame, from the memories and pain of that night, but I couldn't. I wish it had stopped there, but time and again I was forced to get used to that desperate feeling of being helpless and trapped.

Sometime later I was desperate to run again, from another unwelcome visitor – Ray, our lodger. I was seven by then, and that Saturday afternoon when I stepped out of my bedroom onto the landing, I heard another door begin to open. I panicked. I thought he was coming for me, just like he had done so many times before. Within a split second, I made a run for the toilet, locking the door behind me. I stood with my back against the door, breathing in and out, relieved to be behind a locked door. The door handle started to go up and down; somebody was trying to get in. My hands began to sweat as my heart pounded in my chest. Silence…

Suddenly, there was a knock at the door.

"Who's in there? Hurry up, I need the toilet!" Uncle Tom yelled.

I breathed a sigh of relief that it was him. I tried to undo the door, but the lock was stuck.

"I can't undo it!" I cried out.

I was trapped in there until the fire brigade came to release me. It proved a lucky escape – for that day, anyway.

Again and again, I felt I was like a fly caught in a spider's web, trapped and powerless. I was stuck, with nowhere to go and no one to rescue me. When I was eight we had a new family friend who lived down the road from us, but I soon knew him as a molester. Daniel frequently sought any opportunity to lay his hands on me and make his demands. Regardless of the risk, he would also become an occasional visitor to my bed.

I recall one time I was in the living room with Daniel when Dad walked into the room.

"Get down now," Dad said sternly. Looking up, I was relieved to be rescued, but as his eyes caught mine, I felt caught and guilty.

But Dad, it's not my fault!

I could see the flicker of anger and disapproval in his stare. *Why is he so angry with me?* I climbed down from being straddled front-facing across Daniel's lap.

"Move it now," Dad ordered as he opened the door and left the room. I felt crushed.

Ongoing abuse meant my sexuality had been awakened before its time. Attention, in particular from Daniel, was powerful to a needy child. The boundaries were blurred. His inappropriate behaviour distorted my understanding of love. I was so starved of affection from my parents that I learned to find my value in how desirable I was to men. Having fallen into the hands of different abusers, I grew up living as though I had 'victim' written on my forehead. I had no idea then just how vulnerable I was, and how I would subconsciously attract other perpetrators.

I had gone into survival mode, and sadly the primary school I attended offered little relief.

"You smell!" Miss Sanderson's voice rang out with disdain as I approached her desk to show her my artwork. I wanted to shrivel up and disappear. My head was still tender from being dragged by my hair from underneath my bed. I had hidden from my mum that morning because my sheets stank with pee. I had woken with soaking wet sheets after a night of unwelcome attention from Daniel. Mum had angrily pulled me out and rubbed my face in the wet patch before sending me off to school, in some sort of misguided effort to teach me a lesson.

Although Miss Sanderson was ladylike in her appearance and middle-class in her manner, she lacked any sensitivity or warmth. Her harsh words stuck like glue for years and were tormenting whispers in my ears. I could scrub and scrub but still not get that label off me.

While Dad worked hard, it was difficult for the family to make ends meet. It meant free school dinners. No money for a tidy or proper fitting school uniform. Our poverty added to my feelings of shame and worthlessness. I was bullied and laughed at over my tatty, ill-fitting clothes. Being poor embarrassed me and it meant I did not fit in with the other kids. I felt like the odd one out at home and just the same at school. I felt like the whole world was staring at me, as if I stood out like a sore thumb.

Thankfully, I always made a friend or two. Although kids can be cruel, they can be kind too. Lorna always seemed exceptionally beautiful and kind, with a sweet and gentle nature. She was a good friend for a year before we changed classes, and she lived right opposite the little church my mum had sent us to for a few months after some people had come knocking at our home, inviting us.

On one occasion at that church, the man at the front served us with bread and wine and told us we could know God's forgiveness. I felt my heart soften as he spoke about Jesus. I prayed with everyone else, and as I did, I felt God close to me.

During my childhood, I often had very vivid dreams. Most I would forget, but some stayed with me. In one of these I saw lots of sick people on mats, whom I prayed for. It probably happened after hearing a few Bible stories whilst attending Sunday school.

I stopped thinking about all this at the age of eight, as we stopped going to the church and the crippling sadness continued. Not least because the lady with three children across the road had died. I remember climbing up onto the tiny narrow windowsill in my bedroom, trying to keep my balance. I gazed over at her house.

Why had God taken her away from them?

I felt their grief deeply and a fear of death crept in. I looked up at the starlit sky and I wondered where God was to help me as well. I felt completely alone and angry towards Him, yet fearful of both life and death. Any sense of God's presence with me was lost in the darkness that surrounded me at home and in the challenges of school.

My school days were a painful reminder of my inadequacy and deepening inferiority, but in so many ways were easier than being at home.

"Again, again!" our babysitters laughed heartily from the bedroom window. My sister and I had been made to sit on the bench outside whilst they continually poured buckets of cold water over us from above for a laugh.

"It's freezing, I'm soaked!" my sister cried. Up until now I had always felt alone in being singled out. Looking at my little sister now, I felt powerless to protect her. If it was not men, it was the female babysitters that bullied and taunted. They were physically and sexually abusive towards me, continually mocking us, getting a kick out of using us as the butt of their jokes.

Of course, I wanted to say something, but life with Mum and Dad was so up and down with their unpredictable behaviour and constant outbursts of anger, emotion and violence. I had learned to stay silent and just sank into a pool of shame and further rejection.

Memories like that can't just be erased or buried. I hated myself; everything inside of me screamed, *there must be something wrong with me!*

Chapter 3: Troubled

I was ten, and the day we had been waiting for had finally arrived. We were moving into our new four-bedroom house onto the Turnpike council estate on the other side of town. I had mixed emotions. Before leaving the house, I was tasked with cleaning the kitchen cupboards. As I scrubbed the grimy dusty shelves, my mind wandered.

Will I make friends at the new school?

At least I will be away from this place.

With the sound of the horn beeping, my sister and I ran outside the house. Dad helped us clamber into the rear of the open top pickup truck he had hired for the move. As we set off and picked up some speed, the wind blew our hair all over the place and for a moment I felt a real sense of adventure.

This is what it must be like to feel real freedom! I longed for the day I would really be free.

We arrived at the new house, which was much bigger. Its decor was old fashioned, with a psychedelic orange and brown seventies style. As our family had grown to five kids, we needed the extra space that this house provided. I was the eldest, with three younger sisters and one younger brother – Sarah, Marie, Gary and Kim. From as young as I can remember, I had always been heavily involved in helping mum feed, change, bathe and take care of the other children. As a youngster, I enjoyed making them laugh as I took care of them. But that wasn't all I had to do. Some of my responsibilities were to make mum's tea, make her bed, get the kids up, give them breakfast, wash up and get them ready for school, as well as polish and hoover before I left for school. I felt like a modern-day Cinderella: I assumed that these responsibilities and Mum's unkindness towards me were because I was not one of them.

My new school was different from the last. It was a place where I could escape, where I made new friends and felt I could breathe. I was finally feeling accepted. Alison, my new best friend, introduced me to Scottish comedian Billy Connolly and took me with her and her parents to Bristol Zoo; it was a real eye-opener to see how others lived and interacted. We laughed till our bellies hurt as we watched the monkeys giving us a hilarious display of their monkey business.

Despite these positive changes, my home life had not improved. I became increasingly emotionally troubled, and by the time I hit secondary school an overwhelming sense of internal frustrations, injustice and rejection tormented me. The inability to communicate these feelings meant that I lived with a barrage of fear, anxiety, and shame. I built up resentment towards my mum because of her behaviour towards me and my siblings. I blamed and judged her for how I felt. In my mind, it was also her fault that I had been abused, and that even in this new place her new taxi driver had begun to molest me.

I was desperate to get as far away as I could, thinking that running away would solve my pain. One night, when I was about eleven, I lay in my bed planning my escape out of that house. I barely slept that night, and when I heard Dad getting ready to leave the house for work, I crawled along the top bunk and peered through the curtains. It was still dark except for the first rays of light coming with the break of morning. It was still, quiet, just a few birds stirring in their morning chorus.

I grabbed my bag from under the pillow along with the stale slice of bread I stole the night before. Cautious not to wake my sister, I moved back to the window. The rug caught my eye. It had been given to my little sister by her godparents, and Jesus' face was in the middle. For a split second, it was as though he was looking right at me as if he knew me. I turned, quickly opened the window and climbed out onto the garage roof. Making it over to the other side, I slid down the bulbous white pillar. I ran like my life depended on it, not daring to look back. I made it to the town three miles away, exhausted and out of breath.

What now? I had not thought that far ahead. Catching a glimpse of a police patrol car, I darted down a side road and hid behind some bins. With no money, I reverse charged a call to my godmother, who had always been kind to me.

"Will you take a call from Trudy?" the operator asked.

"Yes," she replied.

"Auntie Phil," I stammered, "please can you come and get me?"

"Trudy, what's going on? Where are you?"

"I've left home. I'm at the corner of St Michael's Road."

"Wait there, don't move."

Soon afterwards a police car pulled up alongside the phone box and the officers escorted me home. Disappointed to have been turned in, I arrived back onto the Turnpike Estate and was devastated by the news my dad had been in an accident. Thankfully, he was okay in the end.

My dad was important to me. He was not always easy to be around, but in some ways, I felt close to him. Dad had been through numerous family breakdowns and abandonment as both his biological parents had left him. The pain and anger locked up in him surfaced through silences or loss of temper. I was used to a good hiding from him, but despite his occasional angry outbursts where he lost control, I didn't feel mistreated by him. Most times, we had probably misbehaved. Somehow, I always found it in my heart to forgive my dad as I felt a connection with him.

We had been through some things together, which meant that we had bonded. Like the time Mum left him for another man; I was there with him as he fell down on his knees in tears, heartbroken and sobbing uncontrollably. On another occasion we had no money and had to hitchhike together to the hospital when Mum had a miscarriage. Another time, Mum threw us out of the house – she had her neighbours in and seemed to be having a damning committee. Unsure what we were being punished for, we left as Mum angrily ordered us out of the house and told us not to come back. We roamed the streets until it got dark, our only light from the street lamps. Then we got on a bus and I sat next to Dad, confused and fearful. As the people got on and off the bus, it was the darkest I had ever seen it outside. I was cold, tired and ready to sleep.

"Are we allowed to go home now?" I asked.

"No. Your mum does not want us at home." I knew he was upset, but we had nowhere else to go. We rode the bus until we ran out of money; eventually we did return home.

It was different with my mum. We lacked any kind of emotional bond. She seemed cold, hard and detached. I found I couldn't be as forgiving with her. Desperate for her love and acceptance, I could not understand why she didn't love me, ever hug me or even smile at me. It wasn't until much later that I learned her lack of emotional connection came from struggles in her own childhood. With her father in the RAF, the family travelled a lot, and her father was reportedly an abusive violent alcoholic. I'm told he would even beat his children, making them take it in turns to watch as he inflicted his savage cruelty. All this came out in her relationship with me. Her unkind comments and insensitivity increased and every day it was something else.

"Stop tarting yourself up, who do you think you are?" Mum screamed from the bedroom. "Get a move on, you should have left for school by now!" I was running behind with the chores that morning.

What's her problem? Does she have to be so unkind? Offended and teary-eyed, I shoved my hair into a ponytail. *I am not just a skivvy, one day she will be sorry.*

I flew down the stairs, relieved to get out of the house. I grabbed my long coat; I had carefully cut the lining out of the pockets, which enabled me to smuggle out a pair of shoes I had brought with the money I had stolen from my regular Saturday job. I had become increasingly light-fingered, enabling me to have what others had: decent shoes and a half decent school uniform so I would not be ridiculed.

I hated my life, I hated me. At night I had one dream over and over again that became more revealing of my struggle with my identity. In the dream I would go to school, rip my skin off and there would emerge the person I aspired to be, someone popular, beautiful and talented.

Every time I looked in the mirror, I loathed and despised the person looking back at me, and I blamed my mum.

Chapter 4: Running

"Aargh!" I screamed as I was woken by the shock of Mum dragging me out of bed by my hair.

"Get up now!" she shouted angrily. I struggled to find my feet as she clenched my hair in her fists. Stumbling over my feet downstairs, my mind raced.

What is going on? Letting go of my hair as she shoved me through the door, she commanded me to go and stand in front of my dad, who was now home from work.

"Tell your Dad why you're stood there."

"I don't know," I said, trembling before them.

"You're a liar!" she cried, infuriated by my response. "You're a thief!" Then I remembered the biscuit. "Who said you could help yourself to the biscuits?"

I stood there before her and my dad, accused and condemned. The charge: taking a biscuit. I had been hungry, as was often the case. I was guilty. Evidently Mum had counted one less, or maybe she heard the tin lid rattle as I made her a final cup of tea that evening. The loss of a temper can be a cruel thing. I looked over at my dad sitting on the sofa after a hard day at work.

"Well, are you going to deal with her?" Mum raged, ordering him to beat me. Dad didn't reply. Sitting right in front of us on the sofa, he shook his head slightly and looked down as though he disapproved, but he said nothing.

"If you won't deal with her, I will!" she shouted.

She reached for her new horse whip and began to beat me, pouring out her anger with every lash. I screamed, cowering over, reaching to protect myself from each thrash of the whip. I fell to a crumpled heap on the floor, wincing again and again sobbing uncontrollably. I looked up and stared at Dad's almost vacant expression: he looked tired.

Why isn't he stopping her?

I felt utterly abandoned and let down by my dad. Surely he knew it was not right. I couldn't understand why he didn't do something. It was as though neither he nor I were there. I knew Dad was unable to stand up to her for me.

That week during school I refused to get changed for PE: there was no way anyone could see my broken skin and welts. I confided in Scarlett, who I knew from the estate, and showed her one of my arms that was covered in red wounds.

"That's why I can't get changed, you have to help cover for me," I explained. She looked at me in horror.

"I feel sick. You have to tell," she begged me.

"No way, no one must know." I grabbed her arm. "You've got to promise not to say anything – promise!" Half-heartedly she agreed, and I let go of her arm. I watched her go as she left for netball.

Scarlett broke her promise, and I was visited by Miss Rowan who informed me the headmistress wanted to see me. Terror filled my heart. I knew I was in serious trouble now. All I could think about was why Scarlett had betrayed me. Miss Rowan tried to reassure me as we walked along the long corridor to the headmistress' office. Fearful and ashamed, I hung my head low, my usual posture, then I glanced up for a moment and the picture on the wall caught my attention. It was one of the malnourished children in Ethiopia. It touched my heart and always filled me with compassion. For a moment I was transported into the future with a distant dream and hope that one day I might make a difference.

I dragged my feet reluctantly as I continued along the polished floor, which looked even shinier than it usually did. Miss Rowan knocked on the headmistress' door.

"Come in."

Miss Rowan opened the door, and behind the big, glazed wooden desk the headmistress stood to her feet. She seemed to tower over us all but as she did, she smiled warmly. It was my first time in her office, and I was struck by the beautiful lamp on her desk and the pictures of her family.

"That will be all, thank you Miss Rowan."

I didn't really know the headmistress, she had merely been a distant authority figure, but as I stood before her she seemed to disarm me of my fear. Extending her arm, she pointed to a lady who was sitting in the corner of the room, someone I had never seen before.

"Trudy, this is Sara, she works for the social services. She is here to help us and support you. We have contacted your mum and asked her to come to the school, she is on her way."

As she said those words, I started to tremble with fear.

"Now Trudy, would you please show us where you have been hurt." I stared down at my feet, feeling their burning eyes on me. Hesitating, but knowing there was no way out, I lifted my skirt just above one of my knees, revealing a couple of large red welts. I quickly pulled it down again. Together they tried to reassure me, reminding me that they were there to help me.

"What happened, Trudy?"

No words came out.

"Please sit down." I sat, looking around the office at the certificates and old historic school photos on the wall not knowing what to do with myself. They started to talk amongst themselves, then to me about involving the police.

"We can make sure that this never happens again." The lady continued to talk about pressing charges and taking Mum to court. My head was spinning. "You would need to tell the police what's happened."

Although I was frightened at the prospect of their suggestions, momentarily there was relief as the thought flashed through my mind: this is a chance for me to do something. But then the words of my dad echoed in my ear. *"Your nan left us when we were young, the family was broken up."* It had deeply affected my dad and consequently he had made a personal vow to himself and to me that he was committed to keeping our family together, no matter what. He spent his life working to that end. The thought that I would be to blame for breaking up the family was too much for me to bear, especially as I was the problem.

On Mum's arrival, I was sent outside of the office for what seemed forever and then brought back in and assured it would not happen again. Mum had justified her actions and apologised for losing her temper. The police were threatened but not called, and no charges were brought.

"What the hell do you think you were playing at?" she shouted at me, as we left to walk home. "Don't you ever do that to me again!"

I felt the depth of my mum's anger and fury, and fear took hold of me again. I was never good enough for her, and she made sure I knew it. She was always pointing out my faults or mocking me, angry that she had been called in and put under scrutiny. I was slowly being crushed by the inner turmoil, fear and anxiety, weighed down further by her accusations.

I had not wet the bed for a long time, but from time to time fear would paralyse me and I would find I was unable to control myself.

One particular morning, on discovering I had wet the bed, she screamed at me, "You won't do it again! Take that mattress outside in the garden and clean it before you go to school."

She made me scrub it, and to punish me she invited those I walked to school with to come into the garden to see why I was running late. I felt so humiliated. By the time I was thirteen, I was having regular panic attacks before leaving school. I was fearful of returning home as I never knew what I might walk into.

As the months passed and the panic attacks increased, I told my best friend Tracy that I planned to run. Tracy knew some of my plight, and the day I decided to leave, she walked with me to the school bus stop so I could catch the bus into town.

"Open it when you're gone," Tracy said, as she placed a little plastic shell into my hand and closed it tight.

I sat down by the window and waved goodbye as she made her way back to school. Eager to see inside, I opened it to find a friendship ring, a note and twenty pounds. As I read her note, the tears rolled down my cheeks. Her warm, kind words touched my heart — I knew she cared! As the bus pulled away, my stomach did somersaults as I knew I would soon be on a coach to London.

I had always had dreams of helping those who lived in London's cardboard city after seeing a report about the plight of homelessness on the news. But now I had become distracted with other big ideas about London. I had become even more intrigued after Eileen had told me some of her adventures when she and her friends had been in the city.

Eileen met me at the little café by the bus station for a drink before I boarded the coach to London. She was apprehensive, but she wanted to support me.

"Make your way to Stringfellows," she said. "Tell them you know me." It seemed this was the only place she knew. She walked with me and waited as I got onto the coach.

"A single to London, please!"

The driver looked intrigued and peered over at me through his glasses. "That will be five pounds, please."

I handed over my money, took my change, glanced back at Eileen and said goodbye. I took a seat towards the back of the coach and Eileen and I waved goodbye to each other.

I got off at the coach station in Victoria in the centre of Westminster. I looked up at the big elaborate buildings and lavish hotels with their huge flags outside. Suddenly I felt so small and became acutely aware of my lack. Looking around at the hotels, I wondered where on earth I would sleep for twenty pounds.

I stumbled on a Salvation Army hostel a couple of streets away. There was a vacancies sign in the window. I pushed open the old wooden framed glass doors. I looked to the left, and there sat an old woman on a tatty wooden bench. She wore a woolly hat and scarf that was so soiled you could barely see the colour; she had a number of carrier bags by her side filled to the brim. I wondered what her story was, how she ended up in a place that looked so bleak. There was a foul, unclean smell in the building and the air was full of cigarette smoke that stung your eyes. It was busy with people coming and going, but they looked tired and worn. The men gave me the creeps, but I decided I was not going to be anyone's victim anymore. I headed for the counter.

"How much is a room, please?"

An overweight man behind the counter took one look at me and in a deep voice said, "Single or double?'

"Just a single please!"

"Eight pounds." I handed him the crumpled note from my pocket. Handing me the key, he instructed me to my room. "First floor, and breakfast is served between seven and eight thirty AM. Through that door there." He pointed to a big brown fire door to the left of the reception area. I grabbed the key and headed over, eager to avoid the eyes of those hanging around in the reception.

Early the next morning, I got up and didn't stick around. I stuffed some bread, fruit and a small carton of orange juice into my pocket for later. I made my way to the coach station again; I needed to get out of London. I felt like it would swallow me up. I bought the cheapest ticket I could get, which was a one-way ticket to Southampton for eight pounds.

Arriving in Southampton, I jumped off the coach and started walking. I felt relieved and much safer. I eventually found my way to the pier. In front of the Palladium, on a rock overlooking the sea, was a sheltered bench. This looked like a safe, quiet place. I sat down and enjoyed eating the sandwich that I had just stolen from Marks and Spencers, watching the tide roll in and out. I found the crashing of the waves soothing. The cold, harsh sea air I had not accounted for, but I liked it by the sea. I decided this would be my spot to rest for now and settled down for the night, fidgeting to try to get comfortable on the old bench which had several obvious gaps between the wooden panels. My body pressed through the gaps and wedged into the grooves. In an attempt to relieve the hard intensity of the bench, I rolled my small bag under my head as a pillow. It was a restless night.

The next day I headed into town and stole some books. I had spent the last of my money on a sandwich, but the books would help make a fire.

After five days of sleeping on the bench, I was cold and hungry. It was late when a petite man of Indian origin approached me. The smell of garlic and spice was strong as he sat next to me, breathing his suggestive comments over me. As he leant further forward, he attempted to put his hands on me. I pulled out the small pair of scissors I carried in my back pocket. I lunged at him wildly, stabbing him in the arm.

"You're mad!" he screamed, jumping up in shock. I saw the fear in his eyes as he fled. My adrenaline was pumping; it was a lucky escape. It put me on edge, though, making me feel unsafe to sleep, especially when I heard the drunken laughter of those making their way out of the Palladium and the bars after closing time.

Days later, my legs were so swollen with gout I could barely move. In desperation I called my friend Tracy, and her mum answered.

"How are you?"

I went quiet, all my emotions welled up and my eyes were straining to hold back the tears.

"Right, that's enough," she said. "You need to come home, we want to help you. You can come and stay with us."

I felt instant relief. She arranged for me to pick up a ticket at the coach station and collected me when I arrived at the other end. When I got into her car, she beamed at me and made me feel welcome. I wondered what it would be like to have her as my mum.

Tracy's mum drove us home to their house, which was warm and inviting. Early that evening I heard the sound of police radios and their voices downstairs, so I made a run for the bathroom and locked myself in, wondering what I would do next. They made their way up to where I was.

"Trudy, are you in there? We just need to make sure that you're okay."

Reluctantly, I opened the door and sat on the edge of the bath as one came in and one stood at the doorway.

"Everyone has been worried about you," said one of the officers.

"I'm not going back there," I said stubbornly, teary-eyed. I refused point blank to return home, regardless of their suggestions. Facing the dilemma of me digging my heels in, and the obvious emotions I displayed, the officers spoke with my parents and the social services. The upshot was that I stayed with Tracy and her parents for that first week after my return.

Then dad called me.

"Trudy."

"Hello, Dad."

"Trudy, your mum has left us, please can you come home and help me with the kids? We need you."

"Have you spoken with her, Dad?"

"She won't speak to me, she's been gone a week now."

I decided it was safe to return. I was happy to come home and help with her now gone. I thought that life would be ideal for us now; I believed we could manage without her and be the perfect family.

It turned out that Mum had left home because she discovered Dad had been having an affair. Despite all the problems, though, Dad really loved my mum and was completely dependent on her. A week after my return, he asked me to help him bring Mum home. Against my better judgement I agreed to do it, for him and for the family. Dad drove us over to Rachel's house where Mum was staying. Bizarrely enough, Rachel was the woman Dad was having a fling with.

We walked into the kitchen and Rachel and her husband left us to talk. It was awkward. Mum was sitting in a wooden chair at the big wooden kitchen table. She looked tired and as though she had been crying. I judged her so harshly and saw everything she did as emotionally manipulative. I hated being there; I felt a fraud.

After a while, Dad left me to talk with Mum as I had not seen her since I had run away.

"Please will you come home? Dad needs you and wants you to come home. He is sorry."

Her eyes started filling up with tears as she lit a cigarette. I began to feel sorry for her.

"What about you?" she asked. I reassured her that we all wanted her to come home. It was evident to me that she needed to know she was wanted; somehow, I felt compassion for her. Even though I was still struggling inside, I thought I was doing the right thing. I also knew she wanted to be relieved of any blame attributed to her for my running away, and for a moment we made peace.

Chapter 5: Social Services

The peace between my mother and I was short lived. When she returned home, things soon returned to normal, and within weeks that anxiety and fear gripped me again with even greater vigour. I became a nervous wreck, feeling as though I was constantly walking on eggshells.
My dad worked long hours cleaning in order to make enough money to keep food on the table and pay the bills. We did not see much of him – if he wasn't working, he was sleeping. In spite of this, he was aware of how strained life at home was. One day he brought me a poster home with a poem called 'Don't Quit'. He did not know I had already attempted to kill myself swallowing a load of pills.

In a desperate cry for help I turned to the school, who called in a social worker to meet with me. As children, we were known to the social services. Mum's motto had always been 'children should be seen and not heard'. Consequently, whenever the social worker was due, as kids we were dressed in our tidiest clothes for the occasion, warned to sit quietly on the floor and to be on our best behaviour. We never dared put a foot out of line during those visits, and eventually they just stopped coming.

During my meeting with the social worker at the school, I poured out my heart and confessed to my failed attempted suicide.

"I can't cope," I cried, pleading with them to help me. "I would rather die than have to stay there anymore."

I didn't really want to die, but I felt helpless and desperate. It didn't take much coaxing from the social worker for me to agree to her trying to find an alternative for me. I returned home relieved, not repeating a word of our conversation to anyone.

Several days later, the social worker had made the arrangements to remove me from my home and place me with a foster family. She met me from the school.

"We have a family that you can go to today," she informed me. "I will meet you at the school gate after the bell goes."

"Alright, but what about my stuff?"

"There is no need to go home, we can arrange for you to have some money for clothes, so if you don't want to we can simply leave it."

"No, no, it's ok. I want to go." I wanted to make sure I got some things that were special to me, my diary and some little knick-knacks that were personal keepsakes.

After school, I met her at the gate.

"My car is just here. Come on, jump in," she said as she opened the door of her small red Citroën that looked brand new.

"I only live around the corner," I started, then I realised how daft I sounded. I was not used to driving in a car, and what was more, it meant no time to gather my scrambled emotions and thoughts together. My heart began pounding with such intensity that it felt like it was going to burst out of my chest.

As she pulled up outside of our house, I hesitated as I watched the kids from down the road pass by on their way home.

"If you want, I can go in and get what you need to see you through," she offered.

"No, I want to get my things," I replied, convinced she would not find what I wanted.

"Remember Trudy, I am right here with you," she said in her calming manner. "You have nothing to fear or worry about, nothing is going to happen to you, your mum knows that she cannot stop this. We will not be long; you just simply need to get what you need. I will speak with your mum."

The social worker had an authority, yet a tenderness about her even though she was small in stature and young compared to the former social workers I had known. She knocked at the front door with a quiet confidence, as though she had done this before. My sister opened the door.

"Is your mum there?" the social worker asked.

"She's upstairs," my sister replied, before shouting up the stairs, "Mum! Trudy's home with a lady."

I knew she had been informed and was expecting us. I led the way upstairs to her room. I pointed to the bedroom, so the social worker went ahead of me and introduced herself. As she began to advise my mum about what was now happening, I reticently came closer and peered round the door. Mum was staring out of the window with her back to the door, she turned and glared back at me.

"We've come to collect some of Trudy's belongings as we spoke about on the phone," said the social worker coolly. I could feel Mum's anger. I tried to catch her eye again, thinking maybe, just maybe I'd got this wrong and she did really love me… but she turned her back.

"You've made your bed, now you can lie on it," she snapped.

Her words struck me in the heart like an arrow. Wounded, I made my way to the bedroom that I shared with my sister.

"Where are you going?" she asked as she stood in the doorway, looking confused.

I barely glanced up at her, feeling ashamed for abandoning them and not knowing what to say. My heart was heavy, and instead of replying I turned and hastily stuffed a couple of carrier bags with some clothes. I gathered a few keepsakes as the tears filled my eyes, feeling confused and heartbroken. I hurriedly said goodbye to my little sister. I headed back to Mum's room where the social worker stood outside. Once again, I quickly looked in to where she was, and as I did Mum turned her back to me again.

"I want nothing more to do with you. You're no longer part of this family, do you hear me?"

I knew she meant it, and as she spoke, I realised I was now completely alone. Fighting back the tears, I rushed out of the house with the social worker holding firmly to my two plastic bags that now held all I had to my name.

"It's going to be ok," the social worker said reassuringly. Her words bounced off me. I knew she didn't know what lay ahead. I was determined, though: even if I was alone, I would make something of my life. I somehow believed that now I was free, I could make it. I didn't know what that would look like, but I clung to the belief.

I was desperate to get away, but I left a piece of my heart behind. It had all happened so quickly. The social worker drove us to a small neighbouring village. As we journeyed, she began to tell me about the family I would be staying with, but her words seemed to fall to the ground between us as the tears flowed down my cheeks. They rolled off and dropped steadily into my lap as I replayed the events of what had just happened.

On our arrival at the new home, I was welcomed and greeted kindly by Carole, my new foster mum. She turned out to be a good cook, and fattened me up with her daily three course meals. Carole appeared awkward initially, but so was I. She was not very talkative or emotionally warm, but I came to know that she cared. I was always amazed by her large size against the contrast of her long thin legs! She had long grey socks that dressed them, which were always turned over at the knee and made for an incredible first stocking that Christmas. Her husband, Tim, was a gentle giant. I didn't see him a great deal, as he was a salesman and on the road a lot. They had one daughter, Carla, who was quite shy by nature and well behaved, but she kept to her room most of the time. I never really knew what she made of it all.

They did their best to welcome me, but I was still acutely aware that I didn't fit in or belong to the family. Their home was humble and warm, situated in a middle-class area. They were surrounded with posh houses with white pillars and driveways like those I had only ever seen on TV.

Saffron, a friend from my school, lived around the corner in a nice house. We had met at our school youth club when I was an enthusiastic Madonna fan. I admired the fact that Madonna had come from obscurity and made something of her life. Her influence led me to believe that with determination and grit, I could change the direction of my life.

Saffron became a really great friend. She had one of those fun-loving, friendly personalities, making the world a brighter place with her infectious laughter. She had blonde, permed hair which was all the rage then. Her kind eyes were attractive, and she was always there to listen and to make me laugh. The friendship helped keep me sane.

I loved being around her and her family. Her mum would make a cuppa for us, offer us toast and open the biscuit tin, which was full of all kinds of goodies. She'd sit and chat with us and she made me feel like I mattered. I really looked forward to those times round the kitchen table. I loved the way Saffron's mum listened to us. It was as if she was interested in our opinions and ideas.

It seemed for a while during my time in Thatcham that I'd begun to find my voice. I even started to speak up during my regular meetings with the social worker.

"How are you doing, Trudy? I hear you have been crying through the nights?" she asked gently. "Do you want to talk about it?"

I hesitated and stared into space. I was not used to talking. I felt helpless because I had not made my mind up if I should go home. The frustration and the false maternal sense of responsibility I'd assumed for my sisters and brother was crippling me.

"I miss my sisters and brother so much. It hurts so bad, I feel like my heart has been torn out." I sat and wept, trying to relieve some of the anguish I felt. The truth was I was tormented by the idea that my mum may have been taking everything out on one of them as I was not there. Feeling ashamed of the powerlessness I felt, I changed the subject to another struggle I felt I could not outrun.

"I keep seeing certain things that have happened in the past over and over, and I don't want to, I just want to get on with my life. Now I'm not at home, why can't I just be okay?" I stared her directly in the eye, needing some kind of response. She watched me attentively and as she encouraged me to carry on talking, I began to open up to the social worker and tell her about some of the sexual abuse I'd endured. For a while, I felt safe and now in this moment felt empowered to speak out, confiding in this woman.

"Would you be willing to press charges against the perpetrators?" she asked.

"Yes, yes," I said. It was such a relief.

However, when she came back for the following visit, she had spoken with her line manager and changed her mind about the idea of prosecuting. She began to explain what it would entail if I went to court and urged me to wait.

"We're concerned for you. The thing is we only have your word against theirs, and because of the time that has passed it's not so easy to give physical evidence. That means that the prosecutor and their team will tear you apart in court, are you ready for that? Are you sure this is the right time?" The reasons kept coming. "You are very fragile, you have been through enough, I am not sure you are ready to cope with it. It would be a lot for you."

She scared me. I could see what she was doing, I knew she was putting me off. I felt an overwhelming disappointment; once again, I felt like I was being silenced. Either they did not believe me or I did not matter.

I felt ashamed. I felt as though it was my fault and that was why they wouldn't pursue it.

On our next visit, the social worker suggested I should first see a psychologist, as she felt that it would help me move forward and prepare for any possible future court proceedings I wanted to pursue. I agreed to the visits to the psychologist. They were difficult meetings because I couldn't trust anyone properly. I always felt fearful, as though they saw me through the same eyes as my mum. I felt judged and found difficulty in speaking and expressing my thoughts and feelings. It was like a little genie was sitting in my throat preventing me from speaking out.

After several months of attending, I started to like the psychologist. She seemed young to me, and slightly detached, but slowly I began to trust her. We had started to talk around some family challenges and she was very patient with me. I tended to repeat myself and avoided going too deep into anything as I struggled to communicate and express what was going on, but she was not afraid to keep probing.

One day I sat opposite her in the bare office with its whitewashed walls and wooden desk and two chairs, looking directly into her eyes. I decided today I would begin to talk about the abuse. Somehow, she had begun to prise the lock off my hidden secrets. I started to feel safe enough to open up. Then suddenly, before the next session, I received a phone call. The lady on the other end of the phone told me that my appointment was cancelled and they would try to reschedule for a month when they could find a replacement psychologist for me to see.

"I don't understand. What's going on? What do you mean?" I demanded.

"She is no longer working here."

"But why? She never said she was leaving."

"We will do our best to ensure you can see someone as soon as possible," replied the woman on the phone. "We will be in touch."

I was so angry that they expected me to start all over again with someone else, like it was just that easy! I hung up the phone, furious about being abandoned.

There was no explanation – she had just left. I was devastated. It was such an unexpected blow: without warning, the psychologist had *just gone and left me.*

"How could she let me down like that?" I cried, feeling crushed. I sank into the chair despairingly. I took it all personally. I felt her disappearance was almost directed at me. I could not believe she had abandoned me at this stage.

Having opened the lid on my experiences, I was already experiencing a new overwhelming wave of emotions. I felt tossed around by the waves of a cruel sea on the verge of drowning. I became more depressed and I felt a deepened sense of worthlessness. No matter how hard I sought to escape the memories, I could not shake off the sadness that remained.

Needless to say, I never went back for any further consultations. With Pandora's box now open and the resurfacing of painful memories, I felt more lost and muddled in my inability to process what had happened. I started making really bad choices. So far I'd been the victim, but in a new twist I started to treat others as though they and their property didn't matter or have any value. Deep down, I just wanted to be loved, accepted and to belong.

I was torn with a sense of responsibility towards my brother and sisters. I spent my nights sobbing into my pillow, racked with guilt and wrestling with the painful loss and tormenting questions. *Should I do something? Should I say something? Which one of my sisters would now suffer, or would it be my brother, or was it just me?*

My view and judgement of myself and the situation had been clouded by overwhelming feelings of guilt and shame. I couldn't work it out: now I was gone, had the problem also gone, or would it pass to someone else? I was so confused about what I was supposed to do; the weight of responsibility was too much. I just didn't know if I had done the right thing leaving home, speaking out and breaking some of the silence.

My sisters and brothers were banned from having anything to do with me. After I had turned up at the school to see them, my mum got wind that they had spoken to me. I heard that my brother was now sporting a black eye for speaking up for me. It was her way of taking control. It was more than I could bear. I learned to stay away, but my heart felt ripped to shreds.

Desperate to alleviate my inner pain and unable to cope, I started smoking. I figured my mum smoked in a bid to manage, so I'd try it. Smoking one after the other left me sorely disappointed. I gradually developed anorexia. Food was the one thing that I could control, and in turn I believed that meant I could change what I looked like. I was struggling with my identity, self-hatred and blame and every attempt to escape from the pain left me more and more lost.

Chapter 6: Escapism

Inevitably I found new ways to escape. I was fourteen and still living with my foster parents in Thatcham when my new boyfriend introduced me to the Carters, a large family that had a bit of notoriety in the area. Together we visited Big Ronnie's house at the top of Southend, which had a reputation for being a rough estate.

As we walked into the house, it was dark and dismal and the atmosphere was manic. There was bickering coming from the front room.

"Will you pack it in?" Ronnie shouted at his wife, Julie. "Stop going on, you've already had some!" She was off her face on amphetamines and constantly rummaged in her handbag as though she was looking for something.

"I can't find it, you've been in here," she shouted at him.

"You're mad, woman," he said in a belittling tone.

A guy called 'Lurch' bounced through the door. He was tall and lanky, and you did not need to ask why that was his nickname. He came to do some business and also to pick up a supply for himself.

The house was a bit like Piccadilly Circus; Ronnie had his fingers in more pies than I had had hot dinners. Sometime during the visit, Mel came in shouting at her mum for not looking after the baby properly. Mel was younger than me, four foot nothing, and vocal and bossy by nature.

"Have you been smoking puff?" she asked her older brother Dean as he came giggling to himself through the door.

"Aw come on, Mel," he laughed. "What you so serious about?" He lit up the room with his joyous character, all accentuated by his cheeky smile and swagger. Dean had the ability to turn everything into a joke and was a big kid at heart.

I started hanging out with Mel. One Friday night we ended up at a graveyard down by the Broadway in Thatcham with Mel's best friend and some of the gang from Southend, most of whom were older than us. One of the older lads in the gang pulled out some cans of lighter gas and passed one to a friend. I looked on from a distance as they started inhaling the gas can and passing it around, everyone laughing and falling about like they were drunk. Mel grabbed the gas, inhaled it and passed it to me.

"Here, come on Trudy! Just inhale it, it will give you a buzz! Everyone's doing it."

"Pass it here then," I said casually, as though I didn't care. I was not fussed, but I wanted to fit in.

I took the gas and inhaled it again and again. After a massive head rush, I blacked out and fell to the floor. I woke up completely dazed. Mel stood over me, shouting at me as I came round. *What on earth was going on?* I grabbed the headstone I was slumped against and got up, feeling a bit freaked out with the eerie feeling being around all the tombs. Getting up, I shrugged it off and we all walked away, like we were the cool kids.

Sniffing gas and smoking cannabis was just what everyone did. Southend became a place where I found acceptance and belonging with no questions asked. Taking drugs had become a convenient distraction from my internal struggles, but it intensified my mood swings and made me more emotionally unstable.

The reality was I simply was not coping. I imagined my mind and life resembling a massive plate of spaghetti with each strand representing emotions, thoughts and experiences all intertwined and entangled with one another. It seemed an impossible and overwhelming task to try to detangle and deal with everything.

Then one day my foster parents told me that they wanted to move.

"We want you to come with us," they said. "We think it will be good for you. You can have a fresh start."

I did not want to leave my friends. They knew I was going wayward; I was rebelling against all their rules. I had already started to develop anorexia and was becoming more out of control.

I decided there was only one way out. I planned to try a proper overdose, this time with paracetamol. To be sure, I bought a couple of extra packs at the school shops. After taking all the tablets, I decided I would leave after the next class. I thought I would go home and sneak in through the window I'd left open as no one was in. My foster parents were visiting their potential new home in Cornwall, and by the time they got home it would be over. But as I sat in class, I started to get unexpectedly drowsy. Feeling faint, I slumped on the desk.

"Trudy, are you okay?"

"Yes Miss, I'm fine," I slurred, trying to sound clear.

"You don't look fine. Come on now, sit up," she said, looking concerned.

"I just don't feel well, that's all," I insisted, trying hard to get my words out. She ordered a couple of classmates to take me to the school nurse's office. When the nurse came to assess me, she picked up my bag and put it on the side. As she did, she noticed the paracetamol packets stuffed in there.

"Have you taken any of these?" she queried as she pulled out and opened one of the empty boxes. I just rolled over on the bed. I knew I had blown it and was feeling really weak. The nurse called the emergency services and I was rushed to hospital. The ambulance took off at speed with its sirens soaring. I slipped in and out of consciousness, and on arrival my stomach was pumped.

I woke up in the hospital ward with Tim, my foster dad, gently hovering over the bed, Saffron stood by him. I could see the relief on everyone's face.

"You plum," said Tim, in his kind, affirming way. I caught the flicker of a smile.

I felt so desperate in that moment, but so relieved to still be here.

On my return home, things went from bad to worse. My foster family were leaving, and I had decided to stay. My bedroom floor was constantly littered with rubbish and empty gas cans. I kept using them until one day I had a nearly fatal blackout, where I got trapped in a flashback I couldn't escape. It freaked me out and I stopped sniffing the gas cans.

My friendship with Tracy completely broke down. She couldn't understand why things were not improving for me now that I had the chance of a fresh start. She hated drugs and started to pull away and to detach herself from me as she realised that she could not save me.

Skiving all the time meant that I spent much of my time loitering down the local Broadway, or the Courthouse with Mel. She was visiting her boyfriend Nigel, who was on remand and kept coming up for bail and never getting it. He was a prolific car thief and years older than her. I always felt totally unstimulated hanging around doing nothing; but I was loyal to Mel and went anyway. So, my school days were spent hustling for cigarettes, money and spliffs.

My drug use increased, and I started taking LSD and dabbling with amphetamines. The downside was that when I took speed or acid, it intensified the feelings of sadness and misery during a comedown. Drugs were not what I needed: coupled with my wrecked emotions, they helped make an even bigger mess of me. Although I had grown physically to look like a young woman, I was still stuck behaving in many ways like a child.

In the meantime, I started a relationship with Mel's brother Dean. Going out with Dean gave me more reason to hang out in Southend. It fed my wounded nature, distracted me and gave me a place to run and escape to.

I had also become more obsessed with shoplifting. I'd previously become skilled as a light-fingered kid stealing money for sweets. When I started working on the market as an eleven-year-old, I had my hands in the bag to help me buy my school uniform, shoes and anything else I wanted. Stealing eventually became my 'craft and signature' and a way of making money for years to come. It became an obsession. I was so compulsive that I would steal the same top in every colour available. I could have had four hundred pounds in my pocket and would still steal a pint of milk because the habit of stealing had become a way of life, feeding my acquired sense of entitlement. Somewhere deep inside I thought the world owed me. What's more, I justified stealing from commercial shops with the excuse 'they could claim it back on insurance' and felt it was not violating anyone.

In spite of moving to another set of foster parents, I was becoming even more derailed and was losing sight of moving in the right direction.

It was up at the Carters that I met 'Mad Billy' – that was his nickname. He had just come out of jail for an affray. Dean and I had just had a row and broken up.

"Come on," Billy said. "Let me walk you home. You can do better than Dean, a good-looking girl like you. You need someone who knows how to treat you right. He's too immature for you."

I was flattered, in spite of his cheeky advances. He obviously didn't care much for his relationship with Dean. It was not long before I got swept up into a relationship with Billy. I could not believe he was interested in me; I was still just fifteen. I was impressed by how bold he was in his advances, and how much older than me he was. Billy was over six foot, which made him seem thinner than he was. He had green eyes, kept his hair swept over on one side of his face, and he wore a mischievous smile. He was confident and self-assured but still lived at home and was spoilt for a twenty-seven year old. For a while being with him made me feel safe and protected, as he hid me away and kept me to himself. He tried to keep distracted and keep clean. Of course, using me as a distraction was never going to be enough to keep him on the straight and narrow.

At the time, I didn't know his history. All I knew was that he was fresh out of jail and he was going straight, which was impressive to me. I stopped hanging out at Southend for a while anyway. Me and Billy hung out most evenings smoking hash, until we started dropping trips, doing LSD and then ecstasy as raves started to come on the scene.

Chapter 7: Caught Out

Living with my new foster parents brought tougher restrictions. Cheryl and Steve had two boys, Luke and Damion, both younger than me. Cheryl was very kind and loving and she enjoyed having another female in the home. Steve was a strong alpha male and definitely ruled the roost. Their strictness forced me back to school just in time to sit some exams and consider what I wanted to do after school. I managed to scrape through a few last-minute exams with poor grades.

I managed to work during the weekends but became increasingly rebellious, breaking my curfews, 'speeding' and smoking hash, taking LSD, sneaking cigarettes into the house and smoking in my bedroom. I got caught stealing and was given a warning, but the temptation to do it again was stronger than the desire to toe the line.

This time I was caught on video in Boots by my foster dad, who was the manager. I didn't get arrested, but he had recognised me stealing on the camera. That evening after dinner he asked me to sit down to talk to him. His tone and inability to look at me revealed it was serious. Rather than reclining, he was leaning forwards in his armchair chair. He turned his full attention to me and told me he had watched footage of me stealing from his store that day, but he had decided not to press charges. It cut me to the core. I felt really convicted about my behaviour. I sensed his grave disappointment. I felt disappointed in myself for letting him down, and I knew he had felt embarrassed and hurt. I apologised and stopped stealing for a month or two.

I got on well with my foster parents but our relationship became more strained as my drug use increased. The higher I went on speed, the harder and the bigger the crash when I came down. I was filled with feelings of worthlessness, hopelessness and feeling completely lost, fighting to keep pushing through. I was feeling suicidal again. My foster parents suggested seeing the doctor. He put me on antidepressants, but after taking them once I felt so subdued and out of control of my own feelings that I flushed them down the toilet.

I had not long turned sixteen when I went on holiday abroad with Cheryl, Steve and the boys. We travelled from Cherbourg down to Biarritz in the South of France camping, and I loved it! The hot weather, putting up the tent and the adventure of seeing beautiful new places was a dream. I loved the glorious sunshine, how green the grass was, how fresh the rivers looked. The sea, with its sweeping views of the bay, enchanted me. I thought it was like a scene from a movie. We played silly games of chase and rounders and ate burgers from the coal BBQ, and for the first time I enjoyed being young.

The holiday was only spoiled by my preoccupation with Billy. I had been going out with Billy for the last nine months and although he was now locked up, I was still quite dependent upon him emotionally. He was a prolific thief and burglar, with a major amphetamine habit, but he took whatever drugs he could get his hands on. He also had his reputation for being 'Mad Billy' and seemed to make it his life's mission to live up to the name. He had been in a number of affrays and was facing charges of a new one. It was during my time in France that it dawned on me: I needed to break it off. He was due to be locked up for three years for a stabbing during an affray and I was just sixteen. I did not want to spend the next three years of my life visiting a prison. I decided I needed to call it off.

When I got home from France, I went up to the jail straight away.

"Why don't you just write him a letter?" Cheryl said.

"Yes," Steve agreed, "it would be much easier."

They did not want me to go, but a 'Dear John' letter on its own didn't feel right; I felt I owed him that much. Billy was being held on remand at HMP Reading. As usual, I arrived at the prison gates and was walked through to the reception where I signed in. I sat in the waiting area with all the other visitors, mainly women with their kids coming to visit their partners. The visits were at set times, so we waited for everyone to arrive by three o'clock.

"That's it, line up over here," an officer said, swinging his key chain and just missing his knees as he pulled it up to open the door to the visiting area. Prison officers were dotted around the room so they could keep an eye out for any trouble or suspicious behaviour, especially around drug smuggling. Inmates on remand wore a bib with a number. I could see Billy, number 11, stand up to beckon me over. I noticed how pale he looked but he still had that mischievous look in his eye. He gave me that cheeky smile.

"Alright babe? You look good."

"Thanks." I sat down opposite him.

"Babe, can you get us a coffee?"

There was a little canteen area where you could get snacks and drinks. I came back with the coffee and sat on the other side of the wooden barrier positioned between prisoners and their visitors. Billy got up, leaned towards me and kissed me.

"You didn't bring me anything?"

He was expecting some drugs. I felt bad, I knew he was disappointed but that was not why I was there. I looked him straight in the eye. There was no easy way to deliver the news.

"Billy, I don't think I can wait three years. I'm only sixteen."

He looked at me for a moment.

"What do you mean, are you joking? Seriously, you are just going to leave me now I'm in here?"

"I just can't do it Billy," I replied. With that he paused and then stood up, screamed obscenities at me and threw his hot coffee all over me and followed it with a hefty right hook.

Billy was the type who had to save face and he did a good job of it, making sure everyone saw. Two prison officers came and dragged him away as he hurled his insults at me. That was the last I would see of Billy for the next three years. I made my way home sore but relieved I could get on with my life.

It was the next day, and the summer of Soul II Soul's anthem 'Back to Life'. The warm evening sun was reminding me of the beautiful French holiday we had just been on as a family. I headed into the Cricket's pub where I knew the usual gang would be. As I walked in, Warren caught my attention; he was a bouncer on the door.

"Hey beautiful, how are you?" he asked, with a twinkle in his eye and a big beaming smile that could light up any room.

"Good, thanks," I said with a coy glance, trying to keep cool, "Have you seen Suzie?" Suzie was one of the gang.

"Yeah, they're all out back, in the garden." I was struck again by how good looking he was and flattered that he had noticed me. I had caught glimpses of Warren before when his dad, 'Dodgy Roger' (my nickname for him), was my taxi driver at my first set of foster parents. That taxi had a very dodgy sign, it was obvious it was not legit, but I didn't care: it was cheap and affordable. He was often in the car being dropped to work when Roger picked me up to take me to Southend.

Warren also lived in Southend. He really was drop dead gorgeous, with his chiselled cheek bones, brown eyes, olive complexion and big smile. He looked like a model. It did not take much for me to fall for his chat up lines. I started seeing him from time to time for my own gratification, as it was easier than getting caught up in another relationship. After Billy keeping me in all the time, I wanted to be free to do as I wanted.

Having failed to stick at a college course, I decided it was time I moved out to live on my own and stick to working. I knew Steve and Cheryl were fond of me but it must have been a relief for them because I was high maintenance with all my issues. They had been good to me and I still remember the day I signed out of care and moved from my foster home at age sixteen. I was alone again. I already had a part-time job at the Hilton Hotel and went full-time as a chambermaid and silver service banqueting waitress. I threw myself into the job. A woman who was working with me at the Hilton put a good word in for me and I got a bedsit where she lived. I worked all hours and, when I wasn't at work, I was getting high on LSD or speed.

Occasionally, I entertained Warren. He kept pursuing me and showed me he had a romantic side when he came over to try to convince me to go out with him. He walked in with a big bunch of flowers. As he came into the foyer, he skated with a skid on the polished floor all the way up to the reception, making an entrance that entertained us all.

In those days all I craved was freedom, adventure and living on the wild side. I was always looking for something extra that would give me a high. I found it in drugs and the lifestyle that came with them. Seeking to impress some new friends and hungry for drugs, I stooped to another level when I robbed some people I worked with and the house they lived in. I left my job.

I'd avoided going home to the little bedsit I was living in as I was not paying my rent; I was spending every penny on drink, drugs and partying. Finally, I arrived home after weeks on a mad bender to discover I had missed the news of my grandad's passing. I was devastated because even though I had managed to visit him in the hospital, I had missed the funeral. One day soon after, I came home to find all my stuff on the front doorstep of the house where I had rented the room — officially evicted at sixteen!

After a couple of months of sofa surfing, barely sleeping and staying all over the place, I ended up eventually moving in with Warren, mostly because I had nowhere else to go. I liked him, though, and he really liked me so that helped.

We started to spend much of our time up at the Carter's place, smoking hash or speeding. When we weren't doing that, we were out clubbing and drinking. This kind of lifestyle suited Warren, as he worked as a bouncer at the local nightclub with a South Londoner called Gazza.

I lived for my long weekends, Thursdays to Sundays taking speed and dancing. Dancing was the one place I could freely let go and express myself. It took me into a happy place for a few hours whilst I was high. Other times we hung out at the wine bar or got stoned. I started to lose sight of the future and lacked motivation for anything other than speed and dancing, both of which also helped me lose weight, which I was happy about.

One day we got the upsetting news that Warren's mum had died. She had suffered badly with mental health issues and passed away from bronchopneumonia after an unexpected fall while away from home, taking us all by surprise. The house we lived in was in her name. Warren's dad was a compulsive gambler and soon left the house, taking what little there was. The council said that they would rehouse Warren because a three bedroom house was too big for him. That meant moving, and we didn't want to up sticks, so we stayed and stomped our feet as long as we could. Neither of us were working, so there were plenty of days with no electricity, freezing cold baths and very little food. Our only income was from some dodgy dealings. We entertained ourselves with music using a stolen car radio and bass drum that was an old bucket, with music from

Bob Marley, Neneh Cherry, Run-DMC and N.W.A – all good music to listen to while smoking and getting high.

Warren told me in no uncertain terms that he didn't want me going out shoplifting to make money.

"Babe, don't mess about pinching for pennies. We need the big stuff. I'm on the job," he said. I knew he had a plan. Petty theft and burglaries became a more dependable source of income and we were on a roll for a while. One night, the boys were short of a lookout, so I went with them.

"Here, put on my Crombie," said Warren. I put it on; it weighed a ton. I am sure he fancied himself as an old-time gangster, a bit like his old man who was never any good at it really.

"Take these," he said, and passed me a crowbar and a screwdriver. Crombies proved good for carrying tools. Up one arm went the crowbar, and the screwdriver went up the other. That's how things rolled, it's how we survived.

I got to join in some of the time but Warren preferred to go alone with Daz, who lived with us. On my first burglary escapade my head was cracked when I missed catching a huge whiskey bottle filled with money – my legs buckled, and I was nearly knocked out. Fortunately, slightly dazed, I managed to leg it back without being caught. Running back that night, we jumped some garden fences to stay low key as it was still early hours. Having seen Daz grab something off the washing line, I too grabbed a pair of jeans as we made our way home. Warren grabbed the milk from someone's front doorstep. In that moment we didn't care about anyone but ourselves and our own needs.

Gazza started to hang out with us more; he was a well-built Londoner, a bit of a boy! He became something of a liability for us whenever he was on a 'mission', but we loved him. With the speed came a lot of paranoia and little sleep. One night Gazza stood on our window ledge behind the curtain.

"It's on top! Can you see them?"

"See who Gazza?"

"The old bill, they're on the other side of the field. See, they're shining their torches, they're coming for us!"

"There is no one there, Gazza," I said. He even had Warren believing him. Of course, I knew the CID and the drugs squad were aware of some activities but that was madness! Gazza was tripping out after being up too long. Then he took the knife he had been holding his one hand and grabbed a hold of Warren with the other hand.

"Woz, listen, can you hear them?"

"I can hear anything you want with that knife by my ear, Gazza."

We laughed listening to him. I never imagined then that one day I would end up even more paranoid and erratic than him.

Chapter 8: Anorexia

Six months after Warren's mum passed away, there was a knock at the door from the housing officer. She had the official offer of a studio flat. She stood there with a clipboard and a sour face.

"We have a new place for you, it's a flat in Burghfied,"

"I've never heard of it," I whispered in his ear.

"Burghfield, where is that?" he asked distressed and annoyed.

"It's just outside Reading," she informed us.

Warren began to protest – he was losing the family home and Burghfield was twelve miles away from all he knew.

"You have two weeks to get back to us and agree to take the property," she told him. "It's this or nothing. It's all we can offer you right now – you really have no choice."

With threats of the police and evicting us by force, we had no option but to take the flat.

Warren started work back on a building site with an offer from his former boss Slinky, who was pro-Warren and anti-Class A drugs. Living in the middle of nowhere with no transport meant the only access we had to drugs was when we returned over the weekend. Left alone in the flat every day with Warren out at work, things started to unravel for me. I was faced with being straight for much of the day. After Warren's first pay cheque, I started travelling into Reading every day looking for a job.

During those six weeks before I landed one, I was left alone in the middle of nowhere, just looking for work. I found myself haunted again by the deep sadness and despair I carried.

Even with the focus of getting a job, the troubling thoughts and a deep sense of self-loathing raged in me. Growing up, I had not only held my mum responsible for what had gone on, but the struggle ran much deeper as I blamed myself too. I remember looking in the mirror so many times and wanting to smash it in – and I remembered the one time I tried to, at a school fashion show. I had been unable to look at myself; I was so angry with the person I saw in front of me that I had lashed out kicking in the mirror. Hating what I looked like, I blamed myself and who I was. I despised myself and my anger turned into deep resentment and a refusal to accept myself; I became my own worst enemy. Standing in the mirror now as an adult, I decided to lock that little girl and those memories away. I lived with denial and the fear of facing myself and the past. Instead, punishing myself and running away was how I learned to cope.

On my way to Reading to look for a job one morning, I popped into the local shop where I noticed a laxative medication on the shelf. I was feeling repulsed at myself for eating: being stuck at home meant that I had already been 'comfort eating', but everything that passed through my mouth made me feel disgusted. I had gained a false sense of feeling good from the speed and the weight loss that came with it.

I explained to the lady over the counter I was struggling with constipation. She showed me the tablets.

"You can try these; you just need one or two."

"Great, I'll take them." I bought my first packet of eight laxatives.

With my mind fixated on losing weight, I became increasingly preoccupied with where I would get the next lot of laxatives from. I was hardly eating, just smoking and constantly drinking reams of coffee to keep me stimulated and active when I was not using speed.

The habit of taking the pills started to escalate. It wasn't long before I began popping them like sweets – thirty, sixty, ninety – until eventually, I just took as many as I could get my hands on. It wasn't always easy, as I needed to find new places to buy them from.

I had managed to get a job in Reading with an insurance firm; I was underqualified, but they liked me and decided to give me the job. After months of working there, I started to go to the gym with a colleague, too. Weight control was still my main aim, and I was not deterred despite some embarrassing moments of losing control.

Warren and I continued to work hard and play hard. We missed our friends back at Southend, so every weekend we travelled back and forth to Thatcham, managing to sell enough drugs to keep us in a mix of narcotics, drinks and money for our weekends.

Just after Christmas, we got ready for a usual weekend out on the town. The horn tooted: it was our taxi, and Warren headed out the door.

"Come on, Trude!"

"Hang on, will you?" I shouted as I put on my new Chanel red lipstick. Warren had bought it for me for Christmas. I loved to look good when we went out; I liked to stand out as one with style and I always liked to look my best. For someone who despised herself, I could scrub up pretty well, looking good made me feel better about myself.

After a night of making money and drinking in the wine bar we strolled into Rumours, our local nightclub, sensing the usual aroma of beer, cigarette smoke and feeling the warm heat of bodies gathered together. There was little air ventilation, and it was always hot and stuffy. Even though it was dark and dingy, I felt at home with the familiarity of the place. I always walked past the bar area straight to the seats that were hidden in the dark to the right, where we tended to hang out and be able to have some privacy.

It was a night like every other in there. I did my usual 'hellos' and I dropped some more speed.

"Wanna drink, Trude?" asked one of the usual gang.

"Diet Coke."

"Come on, have a drink."

"Nah, I'm good." I didn't like to drink alcohol when I was speeding. I liked the high too much and I just wanted to hit the floor, where I would dance until we were kicked out.

The bassline of the music vibrated through the whole building. It was heaving, the atmosphere thick with smoke. As the speed kicked in, my heart started beating faster and I had the usual urge to let rip on the dance floor. I was oblivious to everyone else and I got lost in the dance. J came over and tapped my arm,

"Come on, you need a drink."

I was dripping with sweat. The only time I stood still was to do more speed or draw on a spliff. I had a snort and puff on a spliff but would rather smoke the hash when I got home: I wanted to maximise the evening. Being fuelled by speed meant I had the stamina to dance all night, and that all fed into my need to lose weight. I used to wear clothes that hid how thin I was – it did not matter how thin I got because all I could see was a fat girl who needed to be punished. It was a weekend like any other.

Eight months passed in Reading and losing weight dominated my every waking thought and movement. With all the laxatives and the speed to suppress my appetite, I was literally wasting away. I struggled with really low moods. I had lost the ability to concentrate at all and at times was so spaced out and vacant, it seemed as though my brain was shutting down. In some vain attempt I was trying to change who I was, but starving myself and attempting to change my outward appearance never alleviated the sadness or dealt with the inner pain.

It was a cold winter's morning when I left the house in early January, heading for work. The snow was like a thick blanket on the ground. Warren came to the front door to wave me off – he had been laid off the building site due to the bad weather. As I walked out of the house the cold air hit my cheek and I gasped for breath, blowing out small white circles of air. I trudged up the pavement, made it to the end of the pathway and opened the old iron gate before my legs buckled beneath me. I had not an ounce of energy left. I collapsed in a heap in the snow. Warren rushed out of the front door, up the path and out of the gate to where I lay.

"Trude, what's wrong? What is it?"

"Warren, I can't move."

I felt every ounce of blood draining through my body as he scooped my limp body up, carried me into the house and laid me down on the bed. I was exhausted and barely able to speak. I did not move for a week. I weighed little over five stone. Because of our lifestyle, I don't think he really noticed how bad I was until that moment. He stayed with me and started to feed me. I started to eat a little and drink water. I still was really unwell. We spent the week in bed. It was a wake-up call for us – we weren't happy out there and I was a mess.

The struggle was too much and we left the flat and headed back to Newbury. We had nowhere to live, so we agreed we needed to live separately for a while in an attempt to try to figure things out.

Now and again, I would call by to see my family, but I still found it emotionally difficult, especially as the pain of rejection was still raw. I stayed over for a week once, when I came back to Newbury and I was homeless. Gary, my brother, discovered I was using laxatives. He stole them out of my bag and insisted I sit down with him and watch the film of Karen Carpenter. Karen died of heart complications due to having anorexia. I had been speeding for days and could not sit and concentrate on it all the way through. He was desperately trying to grab my attention and to shock me with the story. I was shaken and I was moved by the way he expressed his love and concern, but nothing could deter me, not even the prospect of hospitalisation and death. I simply convinced myself that I was not that bad. In reality, I was in complete denial. The more weight that I lost, the more I needed to lose – it was never enough.

"Come on, have something to eat," Gary said, as he grabbed me a dinner and started on his. "You're as thin as a paper doll."

"I'm not hungry," I insisted.

"You've got to eat something. Even paper dolls eat something!"

I looked at the sausages, potatoes and the few peas on the plate, and it made me feel sick.

"Okay!" I replied, thinking it looked disgusting. I nibbled on the sausage and slipped it up my sleeve in an attempt to stop him going on at me. Sam, Gary's dog, came into the kitchen – that was my answer. I craftily slipped the food to him.

During this time my nan had also died and Eileen, who had lived with her after Grandad passed, now had been given her own small one bed flat. I visited her and persuaded her to let me come and live with her. She was obliging and cared enough to want to help me.

The prospect of being with her and getting closer to her was something that deep down I was happy about. It was a bit strange knowing that she was my mum and still calling her Auntie Eileen. Sometimes I just wanted to hear the word 'mum' roll off my lips and I imagined her embracing me as her daughter, but we did not really go there; there was still a wall of fear around it. Even amidst my craziness, I did feel at home when I was with her. Somehow, we were a natural fit. I saw similarities in the way we were and how we responded to life and I loved her bubbly caring personality.

She was not quite prepared for the shock of how chaotic and mixed up I really was. It made things really difficult for her. I ended up becoming such a strain on her that it was obvious I needed more help than she could offer. I was locked in a tragic addiction. It was such a shame that my limited and precious time of sharing with her was robbed by my state of mind and chaotic lifestyle. I was high on speed most days of the week, erratic in my behaviour, in and out of jobs, and shoplifting all the time. I was also experiencing psychotic episodes due to the strains on my mind and body. I was haunted by the fear of facing the past and the pain… so I just kept running.

By then, I was a physical and psychological mess. I developed bulimia on top of anorexia, so I would binge and then starve. I was up speeding on amphetamines for as long as my body and mind could manage to stay awake. My comedowns off the drugs meant sleeping for up to three days straight to recover. Staying up so long made me sketchy, paranoid, and even more erratic, which meant that I would disturb Eileen, becoming a regular nuisance at all hours with banging and crashing around, taking drugs, playing loud music, and eating all the food during binges.

My worth became based on my weight and what I looked like. I would become obsessed with thoughts like, *I can't let anyone see me until I've got this fat off me.* It was as though I saw a stone added for everything I ate. My perception of the fat on my body was magnified in my mind's eye. I believed that for people to see me like this was too much to bear and so my struggle continued with trying to cope with my feelings of disgust and rejection.

Eileen and I did manage to talk about the adoption eventually. She took out the papers she had from the court regarding the events and accounts that had been given to prove her case to me. I took the papers, but in the madness I never read them and even now can't recollect those conversations, as I was so high. She also gave me a little locket with the picture of a man with wavy shoulder length hair and she said it was a picture of my dad. She pointed out his nose and said I had his pug nose and hair. I cherished it until I lost it a year or so later.

Depression and suicidal thoughts followed the comedowns, and emptiness would overwhelm me. After one of my benders, I was on a real downer and I took another overdose. One of my mates, Patch, knocked on the door. I let him in and he rolled a fat spliff. As we started to smoke, I felt myself slipping away. I liked Patch, he was a good guy, so for some reason I confessed that I had taken an overdose, and he phoned an ambulance. They came to the flat and I was taken to Reading hospital.

I could hear the chatter of a couple of nurses. One of the nurses obviously thought I was taking up valuable time and I was a foolish young girl, and she let me know in her tone how much she disapproved. I felt embarrassed, ashamed and stupid. They wheeled me off to have my stomach pumped. It was vile and it felt worse than the first couple of times I had it done. Finally, I was wheeled out and quickly discharged. I hitched a ride but had to walk the remainder of the twenty miles back to Newbury. I felt lousy and a complete failure.

On my return I grew more erratic in my behaviour and one evening Eileen said she felt it was not working out. I was shattered. I had brought it on myself and I knew I couldn't expect her to continue to put up with my chaos. I was gutted that she had to say that to me, as I knew it took a lot. I was sad and disappointed that even my real mum couldn't help me solve my mess.

Chapter 9: Addicted

As I hit eighteen, I was having more psychotic episodes as a result of a lack of food and sleep. After a two-week binge on speed with no sleep, I was walking through the town when suddenly I felt something unrecognisable rising up in me. I was overtaken with an uncontrollable urge to start cursing people and began to cry out obscenities.

What the heck is that? I was alarmed because whatever it was it seemed like another force, vile and stronger than me, trying to overpower me. That kind of behaviour was not me — it was out of character and felt devilish. Trying to get my head round what was happening, it took all my strength to resist the urge to curse. I battled to keep my mouth shut and turned away from the people I wanted to let rip on. I picked up my pace, cutting in and out of the crowds on the high street. I rushed down a side alley in an attempt to avoid another potential victim, relieved to be off the street. The strange urge died down, but I knew it was something more than me and I felt unnerved. Needing a spliff, I headed on down the alley into Northcroft where I used to hang out smoking and tripping with some new friends. Being down there helped me blend into the background. I didn't say anything about what happened on the street; I didn't want everyone to think I was crazy.

The voices seemed to quiet down after that, but hallucinating became more frequent. Some episodes could last for hours. One night, having been up for a couple of weeks, I started smoking some hash on a comedown. I was on my own and began seeing hippies throwing up everywhere. I was having arguments with dealers and acquaintances that were only in my imagination, and I started accusing them of robbing my hash, convinced they were all there. It was later in the morning after passing out I realised it was an episode of speed psychosis.

I visited my childhood GP. I was on a 'comedown' and by the time I had finished talking, he looked at me and said that I was eighteen years of problems, and referred me to see a psychiatrist. I never went to the appointment. I feared what they may do with me and the labels I would have stuck on me.

I was staying here and there, moving from one house to another. Warren was staying over in Thatcham with a couple, Pete and Jerry, hanging with Gazza too at the time. Pete and Jerry were into injecting speed. Through them, Warren had developed a needle fixation, and he was such a mess that his dad took him over to the hotel he managed to help him sort himself out. I had lost touch for a while. One night I was desperate to get some drugs and I discovered he was at his dad's. I knew he was likely to have some drugs, so I went over to see him and find out what was going on with him. With no cash, I hitchhiked a ride over to Reading. When I reached the hotel, Pete was just leaving.

"Alright, Tru?" I never trusted him – he was using Warren. When I got to Warren, I barely recognised him; he was so thin. I was mortified. He had always taken great pride in his appearance but he was scrawny, his hair had grown and he was a mess. He was cold and behaving off key, like he barely knew me. We went upstairs into his bedroom.

"What on earth is going on? You're all over the place!" I yelled at him. He seemed to be fixated on some junk boxes he said were antiques, but looked a load of old rubbish to me.

"You can talk, I haven't seen you for weeks," he said.

"So that's all down to me, is it? Look, I only came to see how you are.

I don't think hanging around with Pete is good, he is just using you," I insisted.

"I never asked you your opinion," he retaliated.

"Have you got some speed?"

"So that's the only reason you're here," he said. The truth was it was part of the reason I had come. My suspicions and the rumours about him being on the needle were confirmed when he pulled some speed and a kit.

"What are you doing?" I cried at him. "Can't you see the state you're in?" I was gutted.

He got angry with me and lost his temper. He shoved me out of the way, so I lashed out at him and we started to fight. Not only was he paranoid after going without sleep for days, but he went from angry to raging. His eyes were wild, I had never seen him like that before. He grabbed me, threw me to the floor, and punched me in the face. I felt the warm taste of blood from my split lip. As I attempted to punch him back with my skinny arms, he was infuriated and became more enraged. He lifted me and threw me down harder. My head bounced off the floor whilst he straddled me, and even though he had lost weight, I could barely move beneath him. I soon learned that an angry man is a strong man. He was uncontrollable. The punches just kept coming. I screamed at him to get off me as he pummelled my chest and ribs. Hearing the screams, his dad came bursting through the door swearing and shouting.

"What do you think you're doing, Warren? Get off her!"

Trying to justify himself to his dad, he still looked wild but let go of me. As his heavy weight came off my chest, I felt I could breathe again.

My tongue reached to feel the taste of warm blood on my fat lip, pulsating with pain where it had been spilt; my eye was tender to the touch and my face felt sore, my ribs were throbbing. I could barely crawl across the floor. I collapsed on a bed that his dad made for me.

I woke up to a fat lip and the biggest black eye, still barely able to move from so much pain. Our relationship had been truly broken as far as I was concerned – something inside of me that day was completely destroyed. I still couldn't believe he had done it; I thought that he loved me. I knew he was psychotic, but *how could he love me and do that*?

Unable to justify his behaviour, I distanced myself from him. The shock of that night made me pull away – he was clearly a different man. For months we both carried on in our own madness before beginning to link back up together again.

I was still in a mess. The anorexia and bulimia were pacified with speed. In an attempt to sort myself out, I got a little job at Panasonic for a few weeks. The woman who was in Human Resources knew me from my time as an employee at the Hilton Hotel and she liked me, knew I was a hard worker and wanted to help me out.

Warren rented a room in Thatcham and I moved into a room around the corner as it was close to the job. One morning, just as I was leaving after a late-night visit, he grabbed a bag from under the bed and opened it.

"Here, Trude, I am sorry. Look, take these, they're for you."

He handed me some earrings, rings and a chain. I needed to get to work in a couple of hours but needed to go home first and get ready. The house I was renting a room in was locked – they had a curfew and I had forgotten my key. I broke in the bedroom window, left the jewellery on the side and snuck back out for work.

Several hours later whilst at work, the CID busted the house I was staying in. They found the jewellery, discovered where I was and turned up at my work. One of the plain clothes officers responded to my pleas of ignorance.

"We're arresting you for being an accessory to the burglary of a jewellers on the high street of Thatcham. We have evidence that links you to it."

With that, they slammed the cuffs on me, marched me through the building past everyone I worked with and escorted me into a police car that was waiting. It was true that I had some jewellery that came from the job. They had no evidence except the goods, so eventually I was charged with handling stolen goods and given a conditional discharge.

Warren had probably been grassed up by Big Ronnie, as he was the one who pedalled the goods. He had really started to lose his mind due to paranoia and he knew this time the police were hot on his tail. He was so thin from injecting speed that he only weighed about eight stone. I could see his mess and it deeply hurt me; even with all that had happened, it upset me to see him like that. One day the police turned up and he jumped out the bedroom window, legged it over the fields and ran till he finally got arrested.

Warren ended up back in jail, on remand this time. He had been set up good and proper, but again the charges didn't stick, as they had no hard evidence to keep him in. He came out of jail several months later looking for me.

By that time, I was trying to get myself together, staying with Lisa, someone from near the estate I grew up on. Lisa was younger than me and was going through her own struggles but was not into drugs. She knew Warren was out of jail and she agreed that he could stay a couple of days while he got himself sorted. I had mixed emotions about him coming to stay, but we had been through a lot together. I met him when he arrived back in Newbury.

"I've missed you, Trudy," he said, grabbing me and hugging me tight. I was a little stiff; I wasn't able to just pick things up as though everything was okay.

I was relieved to see him looking so much better and wanted things to go back to the way they had been, but I couldn't forget the madness before he went to jail. I hadn't forgiven him for laying into me at his

Dad's. I struggled to trust him or feel safe with him after that. He had changed: he was more accustomed to lying and blagging all the time. It irritated me and at times straight out embarrassed me. I could not help but keep my barriers up.

We made our way to London Road, and he used his discharge grant that he received on his release to score some speed. We headed up to Lisa's. He pulled out a kit and I realised he had already planned to inject himself. I was gutted. I had seen the state of him before he went to jail: not only paranoid and volatile, but so thin that he had to have an elastic band to hold up his trousers.

"Come on, Trude, it will be fine," he said, before taking the hit. "It's just one. Come on, have a go with me."

"I don't get it, Warren. You were so messed up with it, why do you want to do it again? Why do you have to use the needle?"

"It's the rush, Trude. There's nothing like it. Let me give you a hit, you'll love it."

I could see he was itching for a hit. As I watched him give himself a hit, disappointment flooded my heart. I watched him as he poked the needles around his arm for a while trying to get a vein. I soon learned that was part of the needle fixation. I was reluctant, but he was persistent. In the end, I figured I could try it once and see what the fuss was about. He cooked up a bit more in the spoon, drew it up in the needle and put the tourniquet on my arm, pulling it tight. I was never a fan of needles; they already made me feel like I wanted to pass out. After twenty minutes of prodding and poking around my arms, he was getting on my nerves.

"Get off, get the damn needle out if you can't do it," I shouted at him. He had already missed my vein and I felt sick from the needle. I ended up pulling it out and doing what I always did: I bombed it, wrapped it up in a Rizla and swallowed it.

Later that evening, Warren stumbled out of the bathroom and into the bedroom with the spoon and needles in his hand. I sat on the floor waiting for him to try a second attempt to give me a fix.

He staggered as he approached me and knelt down in front of me, slurring his speech then leaning forwards he collapsed on top of me. With all the extra weight and muscle he gained in jail he was too heavy for me to lift. It was the first time I had known him to inject heroin and now he had accidentally overdosed.

"Warren? Warren, this isn't funny. What the heck are you doing? Come on, I can't move!" I yelled at him, panicking.

He was oblivious. I shoved, pushed and yelled hysterically, and as he fell slightly to the side, I began to slap him around the face.

"Don't you dare do this me!" I shouted frantically. "Not now, wake up, please wake up!" I started to well up with tears, fearing I was losing time. With every ounce of strength that I had in me, I finally managed to roll him off me and screamed downstairs to Lisa for help. Together, we dragged him into the bathroom. I grabbed several cups of freezing cold water and threw them over his face and body and gradually he started to murmur and move. I fell to the floor, exhausted but grateful he was still alive. As he came round, I let him know I was furious with him.

"What if you died, then what?" I was livid at the prospect we would have been left to clean up the mess. It wasn't enough to deter him.

In 1992 I had just turned nineteen and we rented a pokey, rundown bedsit on London Road. There was a row of large three-storey houses that had been converted into bedsits. As it was run by some of the Carter family, it was also home to various petty criminals, addicts, drug dealers and families who were on the breadline and had no other option. Some were better than others. The rooms were grubby and rundown. Most of the locks on the doors were broken, the carpets were always dirty and worn, and there were grimy communal bathrooms that you only used because you had to. They charged the earth for the privilege to stay and they got away with it because the council paid housing benefit. Even so, we were grateful to have a roof over our heads and the perk was we got free cereal every morning as part of the rent.

I didn't like living there; everyone was into everyone else's business. Most who stayed there were content with living off their benefits and happy to go from room to room scrounging all day. Then, of course, there were others that did the same with the added benefit of making money from selling drugs or other lucrative investments. Warren began to use this to his advantage by taking the money off those coming to score and scoring for them, only most of the time he ripped them off. I could not stand hanging around waiting for opportunity to knock. It wasn't my style and I couldn't stand being cooped up indoors all the time.

My appetite for speed was still strong, though. I had built up a rampant habit while Warren was in jail. I had learned that earning my own money meant my own drugs and independence. I wasn't happy to be reliant on someone else. I had taken care of myself more than ever since Warren had gone to jail; I had become skilled at shoplifting and knew how to make my money. If I wanted a supply of drugs, I knew I could get them myself.

With everything that had happened with Warren, I had decided the needle wasn't for me. I always thought I could keep myself from going too far off the rails. I'd seen how it messed others up. I sought to have some boundaries. I always let the pictures I had seen in school of heroin addicts put me off. The only thing was the goal posts always seemed to move.

I had lived until now for the fun of being free to do as I pleased and getting high and enjoying myself. To me, freedom meant being free to have adventures, tripping all night, speeding, snorting some coke, any high, dancing, raving, clubbing – being able to do what I wanted, when I wanted, without anyone telling me what to do. Living in London

Road was depressing. I wasn't having fun anymore: there was no more clubbing or heading out with whoever I wanted when I wanted. Now I was back with Warren, I felt restricted. Using and my need for speed had become more of a need to fix myself than a need for adventure.

My increasing frustrations and comedowns led to bouts of self-harm: I would bang my head against brick walls, or off bathroom sinks, or I'd punch myself in an attempt to release all that had built up inside. There was suppressed anger that seemed to find its way out and a temper when I couldn't get what I wanted. The greater the pain I inflicted on myself, the greater the sense of relief. The problem was that it was only momentary. Everything I determined I would do, I ended up doing the opposite. Everything I wanted and knew I should do, I ended up not doing.

There was a part of me on the inside that fought to hold on to a glimmer of hope for something better, I just didn't know how to get there on my own. I could not seem to overcome those oppressive feelings of being trapped by my own impulses and the suppression of my past and present pain. It felt like I was in a car that was heading backwards down a one-way street.

The only things I had really learned in life was to work hard and run hard, play hard and use hard. So, in these early years, although I could get a job for a short while, my chaotic lifestyle meant I was never able to maintain it. I still refused to sign on for benefits. I got that from my dad: he had such a strong work ethic. I had worked from a young age and my pride meant I would just go out stealing. Eventually, when I reached twenty, I surrendered to the system and signed on as well.

Chapter 10: Heroin

We had not been at London Road that long when I had my first taste of heroin. You could get anything you wanted at London Road: cocaine, heroin, pure opium whizz, barbs, hash, weed – it was all on offer.

It was mid-week, and Ricky and Matty were in our bedsit with us. Ricky was a big guy, a gentle giant, his size was often to his advantage. Ricky was a part of the Carter family, it was as though his path was laid out for him, even though he was big he always seemed easily led and a little too nice for this lifestyle. Yet he earned his place in the pecking order, held his position and always acted the big man: being a Carter meant he had a lot to live up to. In this game I learned quickly that people will always take advantage of your weakness.

Prior to that evening, I had been banging on at Warren as he had started to spend some of the money on heroin: he would slip upstairs to smoke it with Ricky. I was happy to be flat out on the speed, but it irritated me that he was starting to spend money on 'the gear', and I was getting jealous. After his third night up there, I was so fed up with him, I told him straight that if he was spending our money on it, I wanted some. *If I can't beat him, then I may as well join him.*

That night, Warren bought a bag of heroin downstairs. Ricky and Matty were there too, and they put their drugs on the foil. Clearly it was not that new to them. Warren carefully placed the brown powder on to the foil he had prepared, then put the flame under the foil to melt the powder and run it up and down the foil, better known as 'chasing the dragon'. Then it came to my turn. I put the tube, better known as a tooter, in my mouth and I began to inhale the fumes. He chased it up and down the foil for me.

It was strong gear and immediately I experienced an overwhelming warm rush running through my body. I had this euphoric moment; everything went numb and warm and dizzy at the same time. It quickly turned into a nightmare as I spent the rest of the evening throwing up in the sink until I eventually crashed out. I woke up thinking, why would I want to do that again? Pay money to be sick? If there was one thing I hated, it was being sick and wasting drugs.

"Warren, why bother, just to be sick? What's the point?"

He just tried to reassure me that it would not last. "That's normal for your first time."

Over the course of the week, I did it again and again, and before you knew it, I had exchanged one drug for another. I had changed lanes. I went from being a 'speed head' to a 'smack head'. I exchanged the high, buzz and energy of whizz for the warm numbing sensation of heroin. It was a 'downer', a depressant: the opposite of speed. Speed intensified my emotions and thoughts, whereas heroin enabled me to forget. Being on the gear meant I was not as active at making money as I would spend more time 'gouging out', sitting or lying down in a dream-like state.

It was convenient living at London Road, as I could get drugs in the same block I lived in. I also lived opposite B&Q, which proved to be a nice little earner, as I could make a good couple of hundred pounds a day by stealing from there. London Road never went to sleep. I never got any peace – it was like Paddington Station up and down the stairs with a constant flow of traffic to our room.

One afternoon, we were in the bedsit when Daz came in with his girlfriend, Della, and a few others.

"Quick, put the news on!" he shouted. It was one o'clock.

On the news, Warren's good friend BJ's house came up on the news. BJ was one of the gang from Southend. His house was all sealed with yellow tape. We all just sat on the bed silent and stunned, watching as the news unfolded. Then we heard the report of a woman being shot in the back of the head and then the gunman shooting himself. BJ had shot Cassey, Mel's best friend, in a jealous rage after she split up with him. They had been childhood sweethearts. He had threatened Cassey before, but I don't think anyone really believed he would do it. We sat in shock. It was unbelievable.

We all got high and gradually everyone left the bedsit. That night, we had managed to get ourselves some pure opium, and it proved a great tonic after the news of the day. After those events, everyone seemed to deteriorate on the gear, for a while anyway, but sadly some of us never came back for years to come, or even at all.

My use of heroin and opium escalated. We tried selling gear, but we were weak addicts and would always just end up using it all. It hit me how bad things were when we woke up one day with no gear, sweating, sick, weak, and barely able to move. This was what I had seen at school, what I had never wanted. I had not planned for this, and the withdrawals snuck up on us quickly. This was cold turkey! I was addicted, reliant on it now to be able to function. I could barely move.

Daz called by with Della and Mickey. He had been trying to score, which was proving challenging as heroin was scarce. We were barely able to move from the bed, so we had a few spliffs until eventually we managed to get a bag from somewhere. A bag of gear for one of us would not hit the sides, as our habits had grown too big. We had been having sweats and feeling ill for the last eight hours and I needed more than a measly chase on the foil to feel better now. I knew I needed to switch to the needle for my fix, so the heroin would go straight into my bloodstream and I could be sure it would be quick.

Warren cooked up the gear, put the filter in the spoon, drew up the brown liquid, flicked the needle and slid the needle in my arm. As he drew the blood and pushed the needle in, the warm rush flooded my being. I took a sigh of relief as I soaked in that feeling. It was better than I thought and I wanted the feeling of that rush to continue. It was always about the needle after that. I began to develop a needle fixation too. I wanted a hit all the time, the feeling of the needle pricking my arm, watching the blood come out and the gear go in and sensing that rushing warm sensation of the heroin flooding my being, breathing a sigh of relief.

I relied heavily on Warren to give me my fix. I disliked having to put the needle in my arm myself; it made me feel sick. Yet as the needle fixation got stronger, I became more impatient and aggressive while waiting for my hit. Warren would often be gouging out or struggling to find a vein in my arm, so I had to learn to do it for myself.

The veins in my arms got destroyed and I was left with couple of deep holes in my arm where I had injected and prodded them so much. I quickly turned to injecting in my hands, feet, leg, groin and eventually even my neck. My heightened distress waiting for a fix meant I was more aggressive, at times like a screaming banshee, and now it wasn't just the drug but the fix of the needle going in my arm which gripped me and had power over me.

This increasing heroin habit made it harder and harder to sell drugs and consolidate any real cash flow. Warren's reputation made him a bad investment for any decent credit. Warren had always been the one to sell just enough to tide us over, as he was slightly better at it than me. The problem was he always ripped people off, which frequently brought trouble to our door, and eventually people no longer wanted to deal with him. I had an insatiable appetite and no self-control, ending up using almost as much as I could get my hands on. This meant that I was under constant pressure to make more money.

My shoplifting became more prolific, and the police started to become more familiar with me. I'd had a good run for a number of years, but now my habitual thieving was putting me in the spotlight. Newbury was a small town with a small high street and I was hitting the same shops every day. Inevitably, with the increase of heroin addicts in Newbury, the shoplifting increased, and that brought a need for store security. It was not just getting out of the shop that got harder but getting out of the town centre without getting lifted. I was slippery but not slippery enough.

Eventually I carelessly got caught for a minor theft in Tesco. I was grabbed by two store detectives on the way out of the shop with some bottles of booze and meat. The store detectives marched me to the back of the shop with the security guard in tow.

"Come on now, let's have it."

"Have what?" There were a few bulges that were difficult to hide – one down the side of my leg, one down the side of my arm.

"Come on, empty your pockets."

The inner lining had a bottle and some meat in them, so I tried to get away with handing some back and keeping some.

"That's it," I said, offloading my pockets. "Can I go now?"

"Afraid not. The police have been called and are on their way."

The police came, and they discovered the rest of the bottles and meat. I ended up in the cells. In my mind it was good fortune that I was carrying some gear in a needle ready for a fix. While I was waiting for the police, the needle was well hidden and not found in the search. In the cell, craving the fix, I tried to take a hit, but had no belt to use as a tourniquet so I couldn't draw any blood. Frustrated and desperate to get out, I pleaded guilty in the interview and got bailed.

Dying to get my fix, I made it to the bus station toilets as soon as I got out. Those toilets had become a regular haunt for hitting up, but I hated the smell of the cold floor and stale urine. The only comfort was the strong familiar aroma of heroin being cooked up just before a hit, and that warm sensation that hit my body and mind, filling my longing for a short while.

Chapter 11: On Top

I was twenty when we eventually moved into a house in Creswell Road, just down the road from my parents. Warren had done a short stint back in prison, and we lost the bedsit. The house had just been busted for heroin; the police's attention was all over it. The house belonged to Terry. 'Screw', the scouser, had been living there and he'd shifted a lot of gear till he got nicked for dealing. Terry moved and agreed to let us stay. It was a prime location to make some money after the recent supply from there, so the agreement was we would give him gear for the rent. My parents lived at the top of the road, so it was anything from ideal. I kept a low profile as I wanted to avoid being seen.

Living far from the town made it harder for me to make quick money and score. We ended up delving into our supply, making us inconsistent to score from. Our raging habits led us to become more distanced from our old friends: some of them had cleaned up, and while some still dabbled, we grew worse and avoided them out of sheer embarrassment. So, we found ourselves living in this house with no electricity and no money. It was the middle of winter and it was dark, damp and cold, which was rotten if you were having withdrawals.

Our room was always dark and dingy. It had a massive double bed and a little white plastic garden table at the end of it, where we cooked the gear. One evening, we prepared a hit, both gouged out into oblivion and fell asleep. As we finished hitting up under the sparse candlelight, we left it burning away on the small metal plate on the table. The candle holder must have melted through the plastic table and dropped to the floor, catching the carpet alight. By the time we woke up, the flames were high enough to touch the ceiling. Thankfully they were contained within the plastic rim of the table, which sat a few inches away from the quilt hanging over our bed. Frantically we managed to put it out, burning our hands and feet in the process as the plastic had melted into the carpet. It had been a close shave.

On my twenty-first birthday I was desperate, sick and miserable. We were at a point where I was sick more than I was well. Living up at Creswell Road was too far from dealers and the shops, especially with no car. With no money to score, we had woken up in the afternoon, which meant I was too late to walk the three miles into town to the shops and I was too sick to go robbing anywhere else. Feeling a bit sorry for myself, I decided to swallow my pride and go and ask my parents for a bath. I still hated my mum – my unforgiveness towards her had turned into deep resentment – but I was desperate and in need of a warm bath. Reluctantly, I headed up the road, rehearsing over and over what I would say. By now, they had wind of me staying down the road because of neighbours' reports. Surely they would not refuse – it was my twenty-first birthday. When the door opened, I explained we had run out of electricity. My mum didn't say much, but she agreed.

I could not wait to get up the stairs and into the bath. That was my birthday gift. I was so relieved just to be able to have a hot bath and shave my legs and feel clean. I was so sweaty and clammy with withdrawals. Deep down, I was hoping that someone might give me at least enough money to score, but of course they didn't. I said thanks for the bath and I got out of there as quick as my feet could carry me. This was never how I thought I would spend my twenty-first. We just about scraped by that night to score; it was a pauper's party.

The next day, I was determined to make enough cash to get a quarter or half ounce of heroin to start us off dealing again. I had just been in

M&S and had picked up half a dozen pairs of shoes, blazers, clothes, perfume: plenty to sell. I had seen a jumper I had fancied for myself when I had stolen a load of things to sell from Debenhams earlier that day. I foolishly went back with my hands full of stuff. The store detective clocked me and my bags, but I got complacent. I felt uneasy but took the jumper anyway.

As I shifted to the door, I saw that another store detective was onto me, so I made a run for it, but the store detective grabbed a hold of my coat. I hurled the stuff and kicked it wildly under a parked car. Unable to break free from the grip behind me, I slipped out of my jacket and, realising the stored detective still had my t-shirt in his grip, I slipped out of my top too! As I ran in only my bra, a police car screeched to a halt. The officer ran towards me as the store detective grabbed me again.

"Yes, this is her, she kicked the bags under that car." They nicked me and put me in the back of the police car.

After that, getting arrested became a regular occupational hazard. I was on a trip around town one afternoon and I spotted a few new undercover police walking the streets. I came out of Next with a bag full, but I felt uneasy, so I dodged the men, stashed the stuff, and as I came back through the alley, they came out of nowhere with one on either side of me and picked me up by my elbows. Of course, by the skin of my teeth I was clean on that occasion, but every day was a risk day!

Shortly afterwards, the bank repossessed the house in Creswell Road. I talked my parents into letting us stay a short while on the promise of us getting clean. My mum was accommodating; I still carried a lot of anger, but maybe she had some regrets. I was so desperate, I would do anything. We never talked about the past.

We had a mattress that was put down in the front room for us to sleep on. The doctor gave us a detox, we got cleaning jobs with my dad as that was the deal, and even Warren did it. The detox was two weeks on lofexidine, and smoking weed helped where the medication didn't. We stayed with them for about six weeks. It demonstrated to me that somewhere deep down my mum must have cared, but I always found myself questioning her motives. My view of her was jaded through all that had happened. Still, there was something comforting about the mattress on their new thick carpet: it was warm and provided some relief from the struggle of moving around. It was a welcome break from my addiction.

Mum seemed to have softened, I noticed. She seemed easier on my sisters and brother now, maybe because she was getting older. By them allowing us to stay, it gave me my first sense of acceptance. One night whilst I was there, my mum opened up about some abuse that had happened to her growing up, and it provided some common ground between us. It was the first time I really saw the person beneath the surface. I felt an overwhelming compassion for her and it was the first time I had felt a warmth from her. However, it wasn't long before something she said triggered those negative emotions again – it did not take much for me to be triggered by her. I always wanted the woman back that I saw a glimpse of that night.

I knew I needed to move out and get a job. I was losing the will to continue getting up in the early hours to go cleaning whilst still weak from withdrawals. I got a temping job at Vodafone and on a bond deposit scheme with the council I got a nice flat, down by the canal in an old windmill. Vodafone then employed me as a Credit Control Assistant. They liked me. I was trying hard to get fixed up, but Warren started slipping in to visit our friends around the corner while I was at work, and I knew he was back on the gear. It was tricky, as he could not stay with my parents. I was trying to get it together and knew it would be impossible to sustain being clean if he was with me. I'd not gone through all that hard work for nothing, but I felt sorry for him, and somehow felt responsible for his wellbeing. I gave into his persistent pleas against my better judgement and let him move in with me. It was a nice place, situated in the centre of the town on the canal opposite the swing bridge, less than a ten-minute walk from work. It proved the perfect location.

I was weak, and soon I was back on the slippery slope. Although I was working, I'd still go home in my break to have a hit and do a quick bit of shoplifting en route. Every time I tried to clean up and get sorted, I would fall harder. I lost my job in the end because I was always blagging. One occasion, I had so much time off at Vodafone, I brought a toy plaster cast and plastered my arm and said I broke my arm. The problems came the following week when the plaster started to crumble and fall apart. It was one of the reasons I never went back. One week blurred into the next and with time everything just got worse, harder and more difficult and I lost the flat too.

Sometime later, back in the madness of homelessness and addiction, I called in to Lloyds bank to see my good friend Saffron on her lunch break. I was sick and a mess. I threw up down my top because I was going cold turkey. Whilst we walked and talked, we popped into Next and she mentioned she liked a red jacket. When we got out of the store, I pulled the red jacket out from under my own!

"No way!" she said. "How did you do that? I never saw a thing!"

Of course, I had my agenda and sold it to her so I could get a fix. As we walked, she gave me her usual heartfelt talk about getting off the drugs, but I was too sick and too far gone at the time even to listen. I knew she was right – she was always right – but all I could think about, all I ever thought about, was a hit.

Saffron later told me, "It was then that I knew that I had lost you." She said she tried but couldn't do anything to help. "I kind of gave up and thought, you will do it when you are ready."

Not long later I was back in the courts, facing another twelve shoplifting charges. This time they felt sorry for me, and they gave me a 24-month probation order. I breached the order and was picked up for shoplifting and found myself back in court.

Chapter 12: Prison

The courts had become familiar with my name now and were fed up with seeing my face for ongoing petty shoplifting charges that were fuelled by addiction. Feeling sympathetic towards me, they put me on an order with probation and sent me to a bail hostel in Reading. The house was full of lively characters – mums and babies, those on drugs or trying to get out of a jail sentence for selling drugs – from young to old, they were all in there.

Warren had been locked up again, which meant it was easier only having to take care of myself. The hostel was strict with curfews, meetings and support workers. It was too much for me to abide by beyond a few weeks. Although I had finally managed to get myself put on methadone script, which I had to pick up every day from the chemist, it didn't stop me still using the drugs and robbing. I tried to keep myself to myself in the hostel: the less anyone knew about my habit and activities, the better.

I had a support worker named Claire in the hostel. She seemed to take a special liking to me. I always kind of felt like she was special, like a gift, almost angelic. Sometimes you see that, even in the ugliness of life, there are people that seem sent to help you or show you great kindness. Even so, I was continually missing my key worker sessions with her and attending the bare minimum of meetings, until eventually I was put on a final warning. I was threatened with being breached which meant the next stop was jail.

It was while I was there that I met Remi. She was loud, mixed race, had stylish short dreads and a gold tooth. She had a hard exterior and she went out with Lisa, who was a tall blonde and appeared more the damsel. One day I heard them plotting to rob someone who was extremely vulnerable in the hostel. That was a bit below the belt for me, so I kept away from them. However, one day after scoring I needed a hit fast, so I asked Remi about selling some stuff I had nicked and if she knew where to score in Reading. I was desperate and had no time to travel back to Newbury. We managed to score that night.

We got talking and she told me if I could get the goods, she knew some shops and market stalls in Brixton where we could make a good earner. So, we teamed up to make money and drugs. I did most of the stealing and she introduced me to her contacts. I did not know Remi's story when we got together. I never asked her questions. We had one agenda, to make money and score, and we both proved useful to each other. She introduced me to a new tactic. She gave me the low down on the goods we needed to get quick easy money. I would go into a shop and swipe the shelves clean of small costly items, straight into the bags. It was quick, easy, and a guaranteed earner. It was a lot less risky, too.

We would jump the train and then buy the tube tickets to Brixton as there was no way to jump them. Most times, the whole thing would take us all day.

One afternoon, we had a bit more time and wanted a bit more money. The market stalls and many shops were closing as it was early evening.

"Come on," Remi said. "I know where we can make some money."

We headed toward Clapham Common and made our way to a plush wine bar and sat outside. The place was heaving.

"Ok, this is the plan: we grab a couple of purses and get out of here," she said. We grabbed a bag and ran. We jumped in a taxi and headed home.

It was always a bit of a gamble. London was always rife with tourists, so the loos were better than the wine bars. Then we would score the gear and make our way home after fixing up. Warren was still in jail, and I was trying my hand with chequebooks and cards, stolen from handbags.

It wasn't too long before my good run at using other people's funds was brought to a sudden halt. I was using a stolen card in a garage, but it was old now and had been reported. The guy behind the counter was stalling me, and as I went to leg it, he put the shutters down. It was all over. I was arrested for possessing and attempting to use a stolen credit card. In the back of the police car, I replayed the events of the evening, wondering what on earth possessed me to go and use the card – I'd known it was hot. Addicts always walk a fine line with the chances they take. In hindsight, I knew it was a risk, but one I was willing to take.

After searching me and my room back at the hostel, they found some weed and a couple of bags of heroin. They added charges of possession and intent to supply, although it never stood up, as it was just two bags. I was gutted they had raided the hostel and got my gear. I was put in the cells and, although it was cold and uncomfortable, I slept well as I was full of heroin that night. In the early hours I woke sweating, in need of a smoke, and pleading for a doctor to get some methadone. The doctor came and gave me a couple of pills. My solicitor warned me I would be remanded, and he would request pre-sentence reports. It was the first time I had not been able to wriggle my way out of trouble. I had breached the probation order, along with the bail hostel conditions.

"You have had chance after chance," the magistrates declared, whilst I shivered and sweat before them. "We are remanding you for three weeks whilst pre-sentence reports are prepared."

It was my first time heading to an actual prison. I was cuffed and marched into the van, past other locked doors. As I walked by, I was curious about who else was behind the locked doors. We came to my cubicle and the officer put the key in the door and turned the lock. I stepped into the tiny cubicle with just a seat and barely any room. The cuffs were released and the door was locked. Now I knew why they called it the sweat box. Looking out of the window, I knew I was in uncharted territory.

On arrival, we were marched off the wagon. There were about twelve of us waiting to be booked in. A tall beautiful black girl commanded my attention, as she was having a complete meltdown. No one seemed to care much about the racket she was making.

"Shut up before I shut you up," shouted a big girl. Another girl started overbearingly rubbing up to her, hitting on her. I realised I was going to need to bolster up if I was going to look after myself. I was not an aggressive or violent person and in fact, due to the size of me, I could definitely be seen as a pushover. I knew I would need to make a stand for myself. My turn came, and I was taken to the hospital detox wing first.

It was on the hospital wing that I met Sheree. She was a North London girl, also detoxing. I could tell she came from a bit more of an educated background, but she had obviously rebelled against her parents and enjoyed drugs. She seemed well brought up and she was a girl who could talk and that took my mind off things. We had a laugh, and she gave me a pair of crisp white 501s; nice, needed and appreciated as I only had the one set of clothes.

After the initial detox, I was moved into a cell on another wing that was along the corridor from the hospital beds. I was locked up with three other girls, and it was a twenty-three hour bang up, with only an hour out to get access to the phone and showers, otherwise it was strip wash in the cells. Even our food was given at the hatch round the corner, and we had to take our trays to our beds. There was no dining room on the wing, so we ate our food in the cells.

One day a week we had access to the canteen, the prison shop, which took hours to queue up and get what you needed. As I queued up, I scanned the place and felt unnerved at the pushing, shouting and carry on. The guards are on constant watch, and everyone wants to know what everyone else is getting. I only had about eight pounds to my name when I went in, but that managed to buy my tobacco and a couple of sweets. We had no TV in the cell, just one another. All we had to pass the time was to clean up, smoke, and talk. I was still detoxing, so slept through a lot of it where I could.

I was the new arrival. In with me was Blonde – she was a skinny busty blonde. She was pretty proud of her assets, looking to show them off at every given opportunity. I thought they always looked a bit plastic. Blonde was in a relationship with Lara, who was more like a tomboy. It proved to be pretty awkward at times. A girl called Dominic was in the cell, too. She was from London, and had been inside enough times to know the ropes. When I found out where she was from, I mentioned Remi. It turned out she knew her and said that a friend of Remi was a friend of hers – she had my back. It felt good to have one of the 'right people' on my side.

My drugs worker Jocelyn liked me, and worked doubly hard to get me into a detox. She secured a place in a hospital for me with the view of going to rehab, as at the time no rehabs were available. I was called back to court after three weeks, and the courts heard the usual sad girl story. Jocelyn presented my solicitor with this alternative, and the courts decided to release me to the hospital on bail so that I could detox and then go onto rehabilitation.

They say those who are on drugs are either sad, bad or mad. The truth was that behind the façade, I was sad. I spent every day covering over the pain from my past and avoiding facing it. I went into a well-known hospital that predominantly dealt with people that have psychiatric problems. They often provide beds for detox patients. It was my ticket out of jail, but it was not a place you wanted to stay too long. There was an oppressive feel about it. Some nights, there were howling and distressing cries that went right through you. The days seemed full of brief interactions with those who were depressed, suicidal, vacant or deluded. I used the common room to get a cigarette and have a game of pool. Conversations proved challenging, and although most had stabilized on medication, some were still erratic. I felt sorry for most of them. It was a long week, and I was thankful I had my own room at the end of the corridor, my sanctuary!

In the hospital, it took time to get my head to focus on getting straight again. I met Big John in the hospital community room – he was a kind guy, older than me, who had been an addict. It had really affected his mental wellbeing. We played a lot of pool together and I told him why I was there. He told me about a rehab called Face to Face and was insistent that I should contact them, so I made a call, and they said I could have an interview. I told Jocelyn, my drugs worker, and she contacted them, but it was touch and go whether they would take me knowing I still needed to appear at court. They decided they would accept me even though I was on bail.

I ended up on remand a few times after that, but never served a full sentence. I always got off with probation, rehab, or a testing order by the skin of my teeth.

Chapter 13: Rehab

I went to a number of rehabs over the years, but Face to Face was the first residential rehab I tried. I spent five months there. Face to Face was in Lymington, Hampshire and it was run by an old Hell's Angel, Marty, who was a former cocaine addict. He was a little intimidating if you met him on a bad day; he was short and stocky with long, wavy black hair and a beard, and he dressed in leathers. He took great pride in his personally designed Harley Davidson. He and his wife Melanie ran the rehab. Its claim to fame was that Esther Rantzen opened it. Marty loved to study the philosophy of the ancient Greeks, and this was what he based his own 'philosophy' on.

I arrived at the train station and was picked up by a couple of staff members. All I owned was a carrier bag that had in it a little skirt Dominic gave me, white jeans from Sheree, and the prettiest vest that I had ever owned. Dominic had given the vest to me, too, whilst I was in Holloway. I pretty much lived in it.

I arrived and was put to work straight away, even while 'rattling'. I was to help with a new building – digging ditches, painting and decorating – it was hardcore, but I enjoyed a bit of grafting and it helped pass the time. I was used to pushing through a 'rattle'. I knew the worst would be no more than ten days.

We took it in turns on 'locky wakey', waking up the house, bedroom checks, prepping breakfast for the house, cooking everything homemade, even including the bread. I never quite mastered the bread – my efforts tasted more like wet dough! If you overlooked anything or were late, you would get extended duties. Once, I left some windows open during a lock up. The consequence was that for a few weeks I had the added pleasure of being on extended duty, feeding the geese the daily scraps. They had one goose, Sansom, who had a personality disorder and issues with aggression; he used to chase me round the pen and attack me without fail! I was only trying to feed them. They scared the living daylights out of me, but gave me plenty of laughs and jokes to tell!

I met my pal Carly whilst at Face to Face. I nicknamed her 'Bob a Job', as she always used to say, "Gi' us a job!" She was a proper 'speed head', addicted to amphetamines, with backcombed hair that she coated in hairspray. She had quite a story: her kids had been taken into care and she was trying to get them back. I loved her. She was hilarious in her mannerisms, and she was manic, more manic than me in some ways, which was saying something.

Then one day, I was called to the office,

"Trudy, can you come here?" Julie, the key worker, beckoned me in. I had already been prepped for the new girl's arrival. "Trudy, this is Sheree. She will be sharing a room with you."

I could not believe my eyes: it was Sheree who I had met in Holloway! Here we were, together again! The last time I saw her she was in the prison hospital wing in a bed opposite mine. Looking at one another, we knew to keep our mouths shut. We both knew if the staff became aware that we had been in prison together that it would be a big deal and we would be separated. She had brought some gear in, so she could not believe her luck that she was in with me.

The staff soon got suspicious and started questioning both of us. I was covering for her, of course. The boss and one of the senior key workers took me into the office and tried to get me to spill the beans, as they still had no hard evidence that she had drugs. I got drilled and lectured about false and misplaced loyalty; they had seen it all before. 'You're not helping her,' was their pitch. Of course, I would not budge. I had learned loyalty from the streets; you stayed loyal by keeping your mouth shut. Who and what I was loyal to was questionable, but the loyalty I had learned was to the end. It meant that I was immovable, no matter how much they tried to convince me. Anyway, she stayed and they gave her another go, but someone got a whiff we had known each other before and we got put on a communication ban. We could not make eye contact or look at each other. We thought it was hilarious. Soon after, though, she left.

Rehab was challenging, but I got on with it. It was the first time I had stopped the drugs and had no replacement drugs. Being clean meant I was starting to identify some of my emotions, something I had avoided for years except when they snowballed me. I realised I had a lot of anger towards my mum that was festering. It was spilling out of me, as though I blamed her for everything, and I was channelling all my anger towards her. One of the key workers advised me to write her a letter to get it out of my system. I never sent it: reading it, I realised I had turned all my pain into hatred for her, like poison on the inside of me. It was so bad that I tried a second time. That attempt sounded a little kinder now that some of the venom was out, but I still didn't send it. Writing it helped alleviate some of that bitterness. I started to try to rebuild a relationship with my parents. There were some steps to healing and reconciliation as I invited them to visit and they did.

As the years of suppressed anger started to arise, I turned my attention to wanting vengeance on those who had abused me and I started to plot my revenge. I told myself they would pay: I would smash their windows and throw petrol bombs in their homes – they would be sorry. This desire for revenge started to overtake me. The next thing I knew, I was pulled to the big lounge in the rehab with one of the key workers and Marty, so I knew it was serious. Normally meetings were house meetings, where Marty would tear strips off everyone until he got to the bottom of things. There were definitely no flies on him.

He beckoned me into the room where a big blackboard faced me, the one he used to illustrate his philosophy or daily philosophical quote. I sat on a wooden chair, which had been placed in the middle of the room facing the board.

"Sit down," he growled in a half friendly tone. The set up looked like one of those scenes of interrogation I had seen on the TV. "Do you want to tell me what's going on, Trudy?"

I knew that wasn't a question where the answer was a choice! As I raced through my mind, thinking about Sheree and another few dodgy undercover situations going on in the house. My heart started pounding. I kept my mouth shut, waiting for his next questions. I was surprised but relieved when he started to ask me about taking revenge on those who had abused me.

"I hear you're planning to petrol bomb some people."

"Why should they get away with it?" I replied bitterly. "They are just carrying on with their lives and mine is messed up." I blamed them for my pent-up anger and hurt and wanted a release. I thought my feelings justified my plans.

After hearing my complaints, Marty took the white chalk and, using the blackboard, he began to illustrate that by taking matters into my own hands, I would end up being the one to pay for what they had done. I was stiff necked and felt stuck in my hatred and desire for revenge. I wanted them to be punished for ruining my life, but Marty talked about spending years in prison. He made me think about what I would lose and how my plot for revenge would never alleviate the pain but could result in literal imprisonment. It was rough! He wanted my assurance that I would not do anything. I don't recall what I said, but Marty really impacted me and as a result I let go of the plan for revenge. I would not go to jail for those people. Why should they rob me of any more of my life? Dropping the idea of revenge did not get rid of the pain, though.

After a while Warren located me, as he was out of prison again. He had called and left his number for me, so the rehab let me ring and speak to him on the phone as a way of breaking things off and moving forwards. He was in a mess. He told me he had to move and was recovering from being tied up and having hot boiling water and sugar thrown over him because of his lying, blagging and outstanding debts. He was going to move to Slough, where his sister was. He had made some contacts and needed to get out of the area. I had decided after nearly seven years with him that I was spent. It was emotional, but I needed the break; too much had gone on between us. I felt bad for him, but knew I needed to end it and move on.

"It's over, Warren," I said.

"Just take some time to think about it. Come on, Trude, you know I love you."

"I can't, Warren, I just cannot. You will be better without me, we're not good for one another."

I felt like a limb had been cut off, but too much had happened. I needed a fresh start. Now I had been away from him for some time, it was easier to make the decision.

Not long after that, I applied for a place on a Travel and Tourism course at the college in Bath. I had always wanted to travel. The rehab let me out for the interview. I was underqualified, but they liked me and recognised some potential. My decision to be honest about my situation was a good move and they decided to give me a chance. I just needed to find somewhere to live.

Once again, the rehab let me out for the day to find somewhere to live. I had no money and no connection to Bath. I got off the train and headed into the council offices. They could not help me, but they mentioned a few local hostels in the area. After roaming around all day and getting nowhere, I arrived at a hostel at the bottom of the pile. I managed to speak with someone who, after an interview, said they would consider me. It was my only hope, but I felt disappointed as I made it back to the rehab. I knew going to that hostel was an open door back into the old way of life. By now, I was determined to try life without the gear.

In conversation, one of the key workers Kevin mentioned a charitable housing association in Bath that might be able to help me. He had come through as a resident and was now employed by Face to Face. His suggestion opened a door for me to move into one of their houses.

I arrived in Bath. The house was huge and beautiful, with a massive foyer and a winding staircase. It had multiple rooms, and occupants with various needs – some learning difficulties, some mental health.

I met Mike in the kitchen. He was a paranoid schizophrenic, but to be fair, most of the time you wouldn't know it. He smoked hash a lot, which is what had made him unwell. His sister was a famous actress who was on a sitcom. I soon started smoking and hanging with Mike, and through him I met Andy, who became my best friend.

The first time I met him, he was propped up at the bar. Mike, who was also a musician, had taken me to the Hat and Feather to listen to some live music. Andy was good looking, with blonde hair and a black leather jacket. He hit on me straight away, but I was not interested. Not only was he not really my type, I really wanted to be free of any relationship. Friends with benefits were all I wanted, and only at the times I chose. I liked guys as my friends, as they were easier to be with, less bitchy. If we could establish that from the off set, all was good.

Andy had a really classy basement flat in Bath and ran his own business, something his dad had left him and his younger brother. He smoked a lot of hash, which was one of the reasons we became such good friends. I hung out down his place a lot, smoking hash and weed.

I got a little job in a cafe and started attending a gym, then saw an advert in the paper at a dance and fitness college called 'All That Jazz'. I had always loved dance at primary school. I remember the PE teacher saying in my report, "If Trudy took everything as seriously as she does her dance, she would be an A-star student." This was an opportunity to fulfil a lost dream. I discovered that my aerobics teacher had attended that college and was a dancer as well, so I took a few lessons with her before I went along to the audition.

I was thrilled when I got accepted, but the dilemma was that it cost thousands of pounds and the school was in Bristol. Andy suggested writing to charities to get the money, so we went to the library and he showed me how to look up those I could apply to and said he would cover the postage of the letters. I handwrote the first one, pouring out my life and heart – it was like a novel. Before I sent it, I read it back. Reading it as a third person, I felt such pain and sadness seeing my life through another's eyes. For the first time I felt connected to my pain, sensing that others might not just see me as a 'bad girl' in need of punishment. I suddenly saw myself differently, through the eyes of compassion.

That night I cried out to God and walked the streets, trying to deal with all that had surfaced. I sent the letter to The Prince's Trust. Andy suggested I write one letter and we duplicate it, so we sent out two hundred and thirty-eight letters. I hand wrote the last one to the Mulberry Trust, as I was living in Mulberry House at the time. I had two hundred and thirty-eight responses, all with a 'no'. Then, last of all, I heard back from the Prince's Trust and Mulberry House saying they were sponsoring my first year. This was it! Things were changing. I still smoked weed, did a bit of coke, E's and speed, but I thought that was cool – I was no longer injecting heroin, so as far as I was concerned, I was clean.

Chapter 14: Sex Work

I moved to Bristol, into a little flat in Easton. It was one of a group of flats in a renovated church that had been converted. The flat came with a sofa and a bed and a cooker. I was ready for a new beginning.

That was when I met Tyrone. He was a petite black guy with long slim dreads. He worked out a lot, a learned habit from his time spent in jail. I had no idea at that time what a pimp was, but later I discovered he pimped out a lot of young girls.

Walking down St Mark's Road in Bristol, on my way home to my new flat, I heard a horn beep, but I ignored it and just continued looking ahead. As he passed by, the car slowed right down, and Tyrone hung his head out of his window.

"Hey!" he shouted, with a cheeky smile that made me think, *you really think you're something special.* He persisted. "Hey gorgeous." Who was this guy? It was too cheesy for me. *Do people really go for this stuff?*

He kept cropping up on my street and around Easton. Eventually, he came with a more relaxed approach and I gave way to his cheeky smile and persistent, persuasive charm, letting him help me bring some stuff into the flat. I supposed he was okay and convinced myself there was something alright about him. The truth was that at the time I just wanted some company. I had been in Bristol a good six weeks. Moving to a new city was lonely, and as I had a few months before starting college I figured there was time to get a few bits for the flat, and time to make a new friend!

I was starting my dream course. It was tough and competitive at All That Jazz, and I was a fledgling student, with no more training than a love for dance. I was older than most of the other students, who were mainly school leavers; talented, young and most of them recently trained. I was there because I was passionate about dance and I was never quite sure how I made it through the audition. I was unable to get benefits as a full-time student, so I worked a little job that brought my cigarettes, coffee and some basic food. The combination of the course and the job meant I was physically exhausted; it was long days and late nights, but I was determined. During that time, I had begun a casual relationship with Tyrone. I fancied the company and, of course, the intimacy that went with it.

One morning, after staying over at Tyrone's house, he offered to take me for breakfast.

"Come on, I know a good place we can go."

"Honestly, I'm not fussed."

"Come on, they do great scrambled eggs. You'll love it."

I thought it was nice he asked but could not stomach the idea. As we arrived and I sat down, he ordered a cooked breakfast, but I stuck with something light. After a short while, he casually dropped the bomb.

"Have you thought about working as a woman? You can make a lot of money. You wouldn't have to keep struggling." With that, he dropped the Evening Post down on the table so I could see some ads in the paper for massage parlours. I could hardly believe it, I was gutted! Suddenly I saw what he was really all about. For a moment I went silent; I looked at him in disbelief, shocked and sickened. He must have seen it in me, and I wondered how many others he had stolen away in this manner.

"No way, you've got no chance! No way, I'll never do it, don't ever speak to me about that again. I'm done, let's go." I marched my way to the exit, furious.

"Come on, what's up?" he said casually as he followed behind.

"What do you take me for?" I yelled, turning back to him. I felt the blow of his words hit my chest in pain again.

"Hey, come on, chill out. You said you were struggling, I just thought it would help," he said in a condescending tone.

"You really think that little of me?"

"Come on, jump in. You don't want to be late," he said coldly.

I got in the car and gave him the silent treatment as he drove me back to college. I felt embarrassed and ashamed to have fallen for his flattery.

He had deliberately been sowing the seeds to get me on the game. I shut him down. No way was a man going to put me on the game no matter how much I liked him. *Damn him, I can't believe it.* I was emotionally caught up; it was that deep need for love and acceptance and continuing low self-worth that meant I always got involved with the wrong guys. The seed was sown, but I decided to cut Tyrone off – I didn't feel safe or trust him anymore. I missed the company, though, as I'd got used to him being around.

Some time later, I was still struggling financially. I remembered an article I had read about a call girl in a magazine who had claimed to have made enough money to pay her way through her studies. She claimed she had a classy flat, nice clothes, money to pay for her education and the freedom to do what she wanted. As I lay in bed over the following nights, looking around at my empty flat and cupboards, I began to seriously consider the idea. In the end I went to the little shop over the road from the flat and picked up a copy of the Bristol Post. Back at the flat, I looked through some of the ads and found that Bristol was full of massage parlours.

Later that evening, I could not shake off the idea of earning some fast money. I was skint and faced major problems with paying my rent, on top of struggling to keep up at college. I picked up the paper again more intentionally, feeling the intense pressure of the worries that came with having no money to pay the bills and feed myself. Contemplating the idea of making quick and easy money was one thing, but taking that first step of contacting the parlour was a huge deal. It wasn't something I wanted others to know about. I felt the whole thing was shameful. *No one needs to know*, I reassured myself. I would just call and see what happened. I nervously picked up the phone, dialled the number, and a lady answered.

"Diamonds, how can I help?"

"Erm, I was just calling to see if you have any work available."

"How old are you?"

"Twenty-three."

"Have you worked before?"

"No."

"Okay, can you come up at three for an interview?"

"Today?"

"Yes, come up the stairs on the side of the building and ring the bell." She gave me the directions and put the phone down.

I had no idea what to expect. I wanted to go somewhere remote, out of the way, and this place was certainly out of the way. I headed over there and arrived at this dingy looking building with the sign 'Diamonds' lit up on the side like a motel. There were some steps leading up the side of the building to the doorway. Every wall of the building was covered in graffiti. It had a seedy look and feel about it. I have to say I was disappointed, as I hoped it would be a bit more glamorous than this. For a split second I knew I should turn away but reasoned now I was there, I would see it through.

I climbed the cast iron stairs, walked along a metal walkway to a rundown old door, and rang the bell. A petite blonde answered. She must have been late fifties, with bobbed hair and large false boobs that were out of proportion with the rest of her body. She let me in, leading me down the dim corridor, where I noticed a distinct smell. I was led into the room at the end where I met Tracy, the manager. Tracy also looked as though she was in her fifties. She had dyed red hair and a pale complexion to match. Tracy came from Knowle West, a council estate in Bristol well-known for its poverty, drug problems and violence.

"I'm Tracy, and this is Liz. I have arranged for you to see a client. He will be here in ten minutes." She gave me the low down on the prices. "It's up to you. For today, your name is Lucy – I actually think it suits you. There are condoms on the side in the room. Next time, you will need to bring your own." She concluded her instructions with a smile. The doorbell went.

It was all happening so fast. But how hard could it be? I followed the instructions Tracy gave me and walked down the long narrow corridor, past several rooms, with my heart pounding. I opened the door.

"Hi, my name is Lucy. Come in."

I don't remember his name. I didn't really care. I led him into the room; I was very matter of fact in giving him the price list, and I took the money.

Afterwards, I threw the rubbish in the bin, went down the corridor and gave Tracy her cut.

"That was quick."

It could not have been any quicker, I thought.

"Okay, you can have Friday and Saturday night!" she said. She must have thought I'd be good for business. Evidently the older ladies had the day shifts. "You will be on with Gloria; she'll take care of you."

Gloria was a straight talking, no messing Caribbean lady. I nodded and just wanted to get out as quickly as possible. I still could not believe that after Tracy had taken her cut, I was left with so little.

I walked home as fast as I could. I rang my dealer, who dropped me off a bag of skunk. I rolled a fat spliff loaded to the brim and spent the next hour in the bath scrubbing, unable to get clean, feeling so dirty and ashamed. I was still in shock; I wept and wept because I could not undo what I had done. I felt so disappointed in myself. They say you don't know what you have until it's gone, and another piece of me was lost that day.

I told myself no one could ever know, that this was my secret. I couldn't shake off how I felt and I kept challenging myself about what I had done. I decided I needed some gear to relieve me. It had been a while since I last had a hit. I caught a taxi to the train station, caught the train to London and then took a tube to Brixton to score. I arrived home about two in the morning. I woke up to a good amount of gear next to me. I knew it was strong and I still felt the effects of the night before. I looked at the clear bag of brown powder and longed for another hit. Fixing up the gear, I was still reeling from the effects of the previous hit, but I took it anyway. I overdosed. Just as I was regaining a level of consciousness, Shorty, a guy who I sometimes scored weed off, randomly turned up on my front door. I was out of it as I opened the door, and staggered to the lounge before collapsing again. He spotted the needle and spoon. After telling me how stupid I was to be messing with it, he grabbed the needle and the gear, and threw the heroin down the toilet, making sure I heard it flush.

The whole episode messed me up; I knew I did not want to be back on the gear. I felt completely defiled after that day at the parlour but continued to work there most weekends whilst still at the dance and fitness college. Having always been quite a sensitive character, I knew I had to learn to shut off my thoughts and emotions if this was going to work. The Trudy I had known died that night and I emerged shallow and distant from anyone. I had discovered from some reliable sources in The Clarence Pub down the road from me that Tyrone had a number of girls on the game. He had no idea about my new venture of working in the parlour. If I was going to work, I was going to work for myself.

I made good money at Diamonds, but working didn't improve my perspective of men, it only tarnished them as all the same. Seeing grown men in nappies or women's underwear was so disturbing, and knowing that they found pleasure in pain made me realise how twisted life can be when you're in survival mode. In me grew a strong, deep mistrust and resentment towards men. I hated working, but I decided that instead of men taking from me, I would take from them, on my terms. This mentality led to more brokenness and put me at high risk. So much of my understanding of sex had been perverted, destroying the beauty of partnership. Working meant I just had to grit my teeth and get the deed done. Seeing men drool and sweat and hearing them complain about their wives made them even more unattractive. Some of them were addicted to sex in the same way I was addicted to drugs. Throughout it all, I would just think about the money to spur me on, and with time I learned to push past it.

Making good money helped me justify working: I could pay the bills, pay my way through college and have nice things now. Drugs helped alleviate the feelings of disgust. I was smoking more and more weed, and with working and using coke and ecstasy, I never quite completed the course at college. Having nice things filled the gap on a superficial level.

I worked at a few parlours but settled down at City Central. It was more money, and it had a reputation for being more upmarket, one of the best places to work at the time. As the new girl, dressed up to be innocent, it was easy to capitalise on clients who were always looking for fresh blood. Some of those clients I would keep for years to come: we exchanged numbers so I didn't have to pay the parlour a percentage for every client.

When I moved from Diamonds to City Central, I decided to keep the same name. Most punters would phone around the different parlours to see who was on, and by keeping the same name, people would get to know it was me. I accumulated regular punters inside and outside, who paid good money. After a while, I would see some of them outside for hotel visits, overnight bookings, and weekends away. Those trips made really good money. The downside was that I was bound by the time and the agreement I had made unless I could get the money upfront. On the plus side, they would buy me clothes and jewellery. Some of them tried to control me with their money, even more so when they were aware that I needed drugs. I just wanted the money and to score. Luckily I always had a good number of punters that would serve me in every area of life: money, drugs, a roof over my head, and as a run around.

On one occasion at City Central, I had sensed something unclean and dark, an evil presence in the room I was working in. I had experienced a similar sense of a dark presence when I first arrived in Bristol, although on this occasion it felt as though something had attached itself to me. It came home with me and I could not shake it off.

After that, I used to see dark shadows in my bedroom, and I experienced some strange phenomena. I could never get rid of it because it was always there and I was constantly aware of the presence of evil with me. It did not deter me from working; I believed the lie that I needed to do it to survive and to pay the bills. The problem was I always wanted more money and enough was never enough. Now, as they say, the devil was on my back.

Chapter 15: Back on the Needle

I met Jake after I left the dance course at All That Jazz. I had been distracted from finishing – well, drawn away by needing to make money and working every spare hour in the parlour. Money was my sole aim! My priorities were having enough weed, nice clothes, furniture and getting the bills paid; I refused to think beyond that, losing myself even more as I shut down and set my mind on the superficial needs. I had been aware of Jake whilst still at the dance course, having run into him while I was ordering a takeaway pizza one day at the Halal shop over the road from my flat. He was like a jack-in-the-box, cheeky but cute with it, mixed race with green eyes and thin shoulder length skinny dreads. He was incredibly confident and seemed full of beans, too, which I found appealing.

Some time later, I bumped into Jake again on the road and he started to chat me up.

"You have a beautiful smile," he said, trying to make me smile. "Come on, let me take you for a drink?"

I liked his boldness, and he seemed genuine, fun and likeable, so we met up and went for a drink together. He came back to the flat to chill out. I rolled a nice fat spliff of skunk weed, he took out some coke and we snorted a few lines.

"I'm not looking for a relationship," I told him. I needed him to know I had not invited him back for anything else. He told me he had just split up with his girlfriend and had a daughter who lived just up the road from me. I listened and we agreed to just hang out with no commitments. After all, he was fun and made me laugh.

We became friends, which then led into more. He loved to cook for us, and his cooking revolutionised my perception of food. One time, he brought a chicken home from over the road.

"Watch this," he said with his audacious self-assured smile. He cut up the chicken, seasoned it with garlic, onions, soy sauce, and some oriental seasoning and popped some basmati rice on to boil. "Here, chop some garlic, cut it nice and fine."

He wrapped his arms around me and put his hand in mine as we chopped and pressed the garlic into a marinade.

"That's how you do it," he said, beaming with pride. "No one else cooks chicken like this." He dropped the seasoned chicken pieces into the hot oil and garlic to shallow fry. It smelt so good, and when he finally served me the chicken, rice, spinach and tomatoes fried in olive oil and garlic, I was impressed.

"It's great, Jake, tastes so good."

"Come on, Trude. It just tastes 'good', is that it?"

Cooking was one of his big passions, and he wanted a running commentary on flavours and aromas every time he cooked. Jake helped me to develop a love and newfound enjoyment of food as he continued to wow me with his knowledge and skills. Following my time in rehab, I had adjusted to eating and now dance and fitness helped keep me trim. Although until meeting Jake I still barely ate enough to sustain me, the intense focus I had on losing weight had been turned to sorting myself out.

Jake was shifting and selling cocaine at the time. He thought he could go unnoticed stashing it in the house, until I took the liberty of helping myself – then he soon decided to stop. He fancied himself as a bit of a gangster because once upon a time he'd had his shoulder shot with a sawn-off shotgun. It was all over a deal that had gone wrong. At the time

I thought he was good for my soul, and I spent more and more time with him.

When he learned I was working in the parlours, he tried to persuade me to stop. Jake's mum had been a working girl; it had left its mark on him and deeply affected him. However, I was independent-minded with bills to pay and credit to clear. No one else was going to take care of things, and I didn't want anyone controlling my life anymore, so I ignored his suggestions to stop. I continued to work, but the closer we got, the more I cared about him. I knew my working was affecting him. He asked me again to give it up. Reluctantly, I gave it up for him and we officially became an item.

Life was good at first with Jake, although I found things a bit restrictive. I got bored of lying on the sofa getting stoned every night. I started to feel my freedom was being curtailed. I wondered what his plan was beyond selling cocaine, because even that had subsided a little. It seemed to me that he just sat around drinking cider, which was his way of coping with no cocaine.

After a heavy drinking session, Jake and I bumped into one of his old friends Leo, who was fresh out of jail. We sat outside the Greenbank pub whilst he rolled a spliff with some heroin in. We got some to bring home with us, which led to us smoking spliffs of heroin every day. I was uneasy about the whole thing. I had not hit up with a needle for a good couple of years or so, other than the blip when I started working in the parlour. I confessed to Jake that I had been an intravenous heroin addict for years and was not long clean. He convinced himself that smoking a few spliffs didn't mean that it would become an issue. I knew myself; I knew I had one of those all or nothing personalities, and it was not long before I was back in the addict mindset. It did not matter how much I smoked because I always craved more. I fought to stay away from the needle, but with smoking it was inevitable and in no time at all, I was back to injecting.

I started to struggle with not working in the parlour. I was missing having money and we were no longer making enough money to pay bills or keep ourselves on heroin. I decided I would try and go straight and get a proper job, and Jake agreed to go back to plastering, which was his trade. I tried working two jobs to fund my habit. It lasted a couple of months, I worked at BT and another telecommunications company. I could handle working and using for a while, I had been there many times before. Even though the hours were long, Jake would often come and meet me with some gear if I ran out at work, especially between jobs.

Jake was not sustaining work and I got fed up with being the only one working all the time and making the money. I decided I would take a holiday to Greece – going abroad to get clean became more of a common occurrence. I chose Rhodes in Greece as I had been before with Andy. I liked Rhodes, and had some great memories of romance and adventure. As soon as I came back, though, I was back on the gear and soon finished working both jobs. Jake was still not working, so as far as I was concerned, this meant he had forfeited his right to expect me to stop working in the parlour. I returned to City Central and started to pick up a few shifts in other parlours, too.

By this time, I'd lost touch with Andy, my onetime best friend. We had been so close, but our friendship suffered and changed because of my hidden secret of being a 'call girl', which affected my behaviour and meant we drifted. Andy ended up back on heroin after linking up with some former university friends. Sometime later he overdosed and died, leaving his young son and family heartbroken. I was devastated to lose such a good and genuine friend. Andy had always been there, no matter what. He was there in my various moves from Bath to Bristol and then to college. It was a huge loss for me and really broke my heart. Jake didn't understand how deeply I was grieving the loss of Andy and thought I was just wrapped up in myself, which made me angry. I tried to stay clean for the funeral, hoping this heartbreak would be enough to push me to get clean. I managed for the day of the funeral but arriving back in Bristol I was so sick, emotional and overwhelmed with grief, that I scored and returned to the needle with a vengeance.

Not long after, I picked up a private call from a punter. He was known to me through the parlour and was setting me up with a website and computer. I decided to let him come to the house. I took the money, he set everything up, and I took him into the bedroom. Five minutes later, Jake steamed into the bedroom, shouting at the guy to get out as he threatened him and lunged for him. The guy freaked out and ran. The fact I had a punter in the house was too much for him. It triggered memories and issues he carried from his past.

After that, the house was definitely a 'no-go' business area for me. I decided to stick to other methods of meeting punters, so I arranged to see a regular punter from City Central at a hotel, as he wanted me to stay the night with him. I didn't tell Jake because he wouldn't agree to it, but the guy offered me an extra five hundred pounds. I agreed, although my plan was to stay for a couple of hours, then make an excuse and leave. Two hours in, I jumped up.

"Graeme, sorry but I don't feel well, I need to go home. I'll make it up to you."

I hurriedly grabbed my clothes and shoes. He was disappointed, but there was no room for debate. I called the taxi, knowing Jake would be waiting for me.

It was two in the morning when I arrived home. I was pleased with myself, getting away with a tidy sum without having to give anything except my time, which was often more of a challenge. I knew I would have to deal with Jake, who expected me home well over an hour ago and was waiting for us to go down to St Paul's carnival, as the after parties went on throughout the night.

"Jake?" I called out as I came in.

It was dark and silent, as I turned on the light there was no sound or sight of him. I walked into the living room and gasped. Every piece of furniture was missing, including a massive sofa, the TV, the units, the lot. As I looked around the room all over the walls, big bold red writing on the wall grabbed my attention: my eyes fixed on the word 'WHORE'. It was as though a knife had been plunged in my heart. I could not believe my eyes; I was speechless, gobsmacked. I felt a mix of guilt and betrayal.

I stood looking at the wall, shocked, imagining what was going on in his head. He came bursting through the front door, bouncing all over the place, shouting and mitigating himself, looking pleased with himself but full of anger. He accused me of putting punters over him. He was abusive and antagonistic. I froze, still in shock, unable to believe that he had done it. The reality was I was ignoring the deep things he had shared, which were now showing themselves through his jealous reactions and insecure behaviour. I was too drug-orientated to see what was before my eyes and simply chose to push it aside in preference for drugs. As a result, our relationship had started to go sour from bitterness and resentment that built up between us.

He really caught me off guard that night. Jealousy made him angry and spiteful. We had a huge fight: I felt betrayed, he felt justified. He lost his temper and he hit me; I hit him back and we fought physically, screaming and shouting at one another. I was emotionally and physically exhausted and I just wanted to score. In the end, we scored in the early hours of the morning. Eventually after we'd had a hit, he confessed he had stashed my furniture outside in the rubbish area that was sealed off.

There was an endless battle between us about me working; he liked the drugs but resented me selling my body. Our habits increased, we fought more, and I was coming off worse and worse. The fighting was getting more intense physically. We would literally batter each other. Our relationship became deeply broken and highly toxic.

One morning I awoke 'rattling' and went to the toilet. I suddenly felt a massive pain as I sat down, and I passed something into the pan. I looked down and realised it contained a tiny foetus. I could not believe my eyes. I was devastated. I had never been able to get pregnant before, not that I had tried to with the way my life was, but faced with the loss of this little one I felt completely gutted and realised just how precious life is. For a moment I thought about Eileen, who could have had an abortion, and although life felt like hell, in that moment I was grateful to be alive. As I looked down the toilet, it was more than I could bear. I quickly flushed the toilet to try to erase what just happened. I never told anyone, thinking if I didn't acknowledge it maybe it would be erased forever.

During this time, crack had also come on the scene and was rampant in Easton. I had always avoided crack. It was rife in London and I saw how it affected the girls and burnt a hole in the pocket. Sometimes, Remi would encourage me to have a snowball, a mix of crack and heroin together in the needle, but it was a treat in those days. I was so bothered about my supply of heroin that I barely gave way to a snowball.

Then one night Jake came bursting through the door. The vibe was intense; he was a bit sketchy and eager to open the little piece of silver foil in his hands. His face became serious as his attention focused on getting set up for a smoke.

"Light another fag Trude," he said, making his way to the kitchen sideboard. "I've got us a stone." Unable to take his time, he eagerly lit another cigarette for ash. He let it burn away as he took a can of beer, pierced some holes in it, then covered it with ash and broke a piece off the stone.

I remembered the girls I had met in London who smoked a lot of crack, how it had messed them up so badly. *It's just a smoke, Trude,* I told myself. I took the pipe to my mouth and put the flame to the little white stone sitting on the ash, inhaling the smoke with its distinct smell of the ammonia, which they mix the cocaine with. As I inhaled and breathed out, my heart rate increased and a feeling of ecstasy hit me. It stimulated such a high that the intense feelings of pleasure blew my mind and raced through my body. Within a couple of minutes, I wanted another go. That's how it is with crack: the minute the ecstasy drops, you want to experience it again, and it is never enough. A stone barely gives you two decent pipes each. You need the gear to bring you down and settle you.

My appetite grew fast and was insatiable. Things quickly snowballed. Crack ripped its way into our lives like a hurricane; it ravished me and saw us destroy each other. Violence, aggression and paranoia ruined our relationship even more. Our drive for drugs always took over and came first. I was a slave again to heroin, and now the crack pipe had gained its grip on me too.

Around that time, I had news of my sister getting married. I'd had a week to prepare to go. I had missed my other siblings' weddings, so I was determined to make this one. Still, when it came to it, I barely had any money, just enough that I managed to score some drugs and keep a little for the train. It was the first time I could remember wanting to put something before money and drugs. Jake and I got into a fight over it. We had a full-scale row and it got really violent. I came off worse, and ended up in a heap at the end of the path, completely exhausted. I had missed the train and was emotionally wiped out. I never made it.

The addiction ruled us: the violence just left me more broken and made me throw myself even more into getting high. Smoking crack caused me to lose everything and with it, myself. I always wanted the next hit, or the money for the next hit – it was relentless. I went from being obsessed to being possessed. I had sold everything in the house that I could, even the clothes on my back.

Chapter 16: Working the Streets

One early morning, I arrived home around three after working in the parlour. I rang my dealer and paid off the debt we owed, then scored again. Smoking crack left me struggling to keep up. The money was going up in smoke as quick as I could make it.

In the early hours of that morning, Leo came around to the flat. Since coming out of jail, he'd found where we lived and become a nuisance and imposed himself on us. Leo at the time was big in 'talk', big in size and big on intimidation. He was easily five times the size of Jake. This time he had Shelley, a working girl, with him. As the night went on Leo started to 'switch'. Smoking crack made him increasingly paranoid and aggressive as he smoked. I did not like having him in the flat, and I blamed Jake for letting him in. I knew that Jake was unsettled by him at times and Leo played on it, using threats or attempts to break down the door to get in.

By half past four in the morning, Leo had barricaded the front door and was sitting at the letter box with a knife in his hands. His extreme paranoia meant his behaviour was intimidating. He brought a dark, uncomfortable vibe that made us all uneasy and ruined everyone's night. Meanwhile I was scratching around as usual for any little bits of crack cocaine that I was convinced had dropped in the ashtray, on the sofa or on the floor.

Suddenly, after being quiet for almost an hour, Shelley piped up boldly to Leo that she was getting ready to go and work the streets in half an hour. Leo didn't argue and gradually he moved himself and all the stuff away from the door – of course, he hoped to get a smoke off the back of her working. I asked Shelley about what it was like working the streets, what she did, where she went, and what she charged.

Up until now, I never imagined myself working on the streets, but I was tempted by the quick cash. She made it sound so easy and her answers persuaded me. I needed to get out of the flat, anyway. Leo had done my head in and ruined the vibe.

"Ok," I said, making a snap decision. "I'm going out with Shelley." Jake had been fairly quiet up until now.

"No, you don't need to go," he said.

"Come on, we need some gear. How do you think I'll be able to get to work tonight, especially if I am sick?"

He went quiet; he knew it would be a struggle. Having spent all the money and with only a tiny bit of heroin stashed away from Leo's prying eyes, I had no chequebooks or cards to use. I had not shoplifted for ages, especially since working the parlours, as I always made decent money. Jake gave in. I told him it would just be a one off.

Shelley and I left the flat at around half past five in the morning, which was prime time to catch the punters before they went to work or came back from night shifts. We walked up to Warwick Road, a few minutes' walk from my flat. Warwick Road was one of the popular places for the working girls to go and we were the first girls on the street that morning.

"Which corner do you want?" Shelley asked, pointing to the different street corners. I took a glance around.

"I don't mind. Up there I think?" I pointed to the top of the road. It appeared the least obvious corner; the darkness seemed to overshadow it.

As I made my way up the road to the street corner, I began to feel uncomfortable. I felt so exposed, although thankfully it was winter, so it was still dark. As I got halfway up the road, a car slowed down and crept up alongside me. The driver was obviously a punter, I looked at him and he smiled at me.

"I haven't seen you before," he said.

"That's because you haven't, are you looking?" I asked, looking him straight in the eye.

"Yes, how much?" he replied.

"Well, that depends on what you want."

We agreed a price and he opened the door and invited me to jump in. As I got in and closed the door, he said he wanted to drive to his usual quiet place.

"Where is it?"

"Look, I don't want to get caught," he said confidently. Shelley had said nothing about driving out of the area, but I understood his rationale. I didn't like the sound of it, though – it made me anxious and put me on edge. I played it cool, not letting on I was worried. I was used to the safety net of the parlours. I didn't even know this guy, what if he was to switch? I knew if I let him go now that I may not make any money. It was getting later and I was desperate for the cash to score. I refused to go home empty handed.

My senses were heightened and I was on red alert as we drove. I was with a complete stranger driving to a place I had no clue about. Panic set in and every fear imaginable was racing through my head. Now I had picked him up, I just wanted to get the job done and get back home to have a hit. Stark fear gripped me and my palms began to sweat as I began to consider if I would come back alive; I knew anything could happen. As we drove, I had to keep calm, reassuring myself it would be okay, rehearsing a getaway plan, reminding myself I had a phone.

I wanted to be in control but he was the one driving the car, and I had no idea where we were going. I did not like feeling powerless and had a strong sense that my safety was threatened.

Having finally arrived, it took no time, and I couldn't understand why we had needed to travel so far. It took ages driving back through the traffic, and I was relieved to finally be able to leave the car. I thought to myself that next time I would call the shots. He dropped me back at Warwick Road. There was no sign of Shelley, and I wasn't going to hang around now that it was getting light. We had agreed to meet up after we had finished, but I just wanted to get off the street and get a hit after what had just happened. As I walked home, I knew I would just have to push past the feelings of fear if I was ever to work outside again.

The quick extra money appealed to me and I started working the streets in the early hours of the morning after a shift in the parlour. With my habit ever increasing, at least I now had the option to work the streets as well as the parlours. Discretion was no longer an issue. I could pick up almost any time – of course, there were peak times, but all the same, there was always someone. I picked up some 'decent' clients on the road that paid reasonable money, and the perk was that I didn't have to hand any of it over. There was also the bonus that I did not have to sit in a parlour for six to twelve hours. There were always those punters that wanted to pay less than the parlours, but in the early days it balanced out. Private clients from the parlours paid bigger money when I met up with them outside. Not only was working freelance quicker, but I could get a smoke and hit in between jobs.

After a few years on the street robbing or ripping off a number of clients, I burned my bridges. I lost some along the way when they caught onto my tricks or discovered a clean bank account where I had robbed them. I didn't mind as in the end the demands of regulars on my time were more than I wanted to give. Knowing that I had robbed someone of their savings pricked my conscience from time to time, but the overwhelming desire to use meant I justified it as a means to an end. I would push it out of my mind and get on with finding another source of income.

Smoking crack constantly, injecting heroin at every opportunity, and staying out working night after night took its toll on me. My appearance and behaviour deteriorated, and it was becoming increasingly difficult to mask. Everyone in City Central could see I was on something: I had lost loads of weight, it showed in my eyes, my face and in my attitude. I had always managed my habit to a point where nobody questioned me, as I could still function. Now my behaviour was obviously erratic. I was continually restless, up and down, on edge and scratching around for crack. Having sneaky hits on the pipe meant I was not only fidgeting constantly, getting paranoid and wanting a hit of gear, but I would also pace back and forth or get fixated with looking in the mirror and picking my face. My ability to relax and wait patiently until the end of a shift was no longer there – as soon as I had a client and made money I wanted to leave to go and score. The usual waiting of six to eight hours or more had become more than I could bear. Eventually the parlour manager took me aside and told me to sort myself out otherwise she would have to let me go. A few weeks later, myself and another girl got caught up in a robbery that took place in the parlour. I left after that night and never went back.

Chapter 17: Out of Control

Working constantly meant weeks without proper sleep, which left me paranoid, scatty, and ruthless. I got more careless in my attitude and became greedier but I was too tired to think straight and make sharp decisions.

On one occasion, after three weeks of being up, I had been using a dodgy credit card again. I had got away with it several times but this particular day a warning bell rang inside me. The branch I intended to use was only at the bottom of my road. I ignored the red flags, as always. I was scamming someone else's account in the same bank I had often used for my own account. Instead of going out of the area, I had become complacent and had enquired about a loan that was being considered. I had been hammering it all week, and the card was getting old. Just the day before, I had walked up to the cashier behind the screen, and his stare made me a little anxious, so I quickly pointed to the cashier nearby and said she knows me. The cashier nodded in agreement, as it was my bank!

Rather than heeding the warning, the urge to score clouded my judgement. As I tried to make the transaction the next day, I felt the cashier was taking too long. I tried to hold out to be sure, but suddenly I knew I had to make a run for it. I darted for the door but it was too late, the security man practically covered the door from one side of the frame to the other, and there was no getting past him. The shutters came down and security grabbed me and escorted me upstairs until the police came. I got bailed again; I had jumped bail so many times that I couldn't understand why they still gave it to me.

Over time, the streets became my home. I would be on the street more than at home. It drove Jake nuts! Have you heard of men putting women on the streets? That was not my story. Jake was trying to get me off the street. At the start I think he was torn because he had a habit too. Maybe he would have coped better if I had made room for him, but the only thing I cared about now was money and drugs. I was blinded by my own need, and greed. His frustration came out in violence.

Once, in the early hours of the morning, I was working at the lower end of Warwick Road. Jake came storming up the road, shouting at me. He was fed up with me not sleeping; it was weeks since I'd had proper sleep.

"Why don't you just come to bed?" he screamed at me. "I just want you to come to bed!"

Sleep. I'd forgotten what that was. I didn't want to go to bed. I preferred to keep going – keep working, keep smoking crack, keep injecting heroin. I had no desire to lie down and I lived only to take care of my habit.

"Jake, move! You're stopping me from picking up any punters," I replied. He made me so angry. Didn't he know I was trying to work? I started to get desperate. "Move! Just go home and I'll come after, just get out of the road!"

The cars started to swerve around him as he literally stood in the middle of the street, obstructing the cars coming down the road. He was drawing attention to us and making it impossible for me to pick up. I just wanted a hit but he was screaming for my attention. Eventually, he left me no choice. I had to walk away from my street corner that afternoon, infuriated and defeated by his persistence.

I had tried to get clean so many times. At one point, one of the bosses at a new parlour I was at, Dexter, sympathised with me. The parlour there was a bit more run down, but Dexter agreed to let me detox in their underground cellar, kitted out as a dungeon. I stayed down there for five days to get clean. It was in his interest, as I could make some good money if I cleaned up. I could barely muster up the energy to walk home the day I left, feeling weak and tired – normal for five days into a detox. Despite my good intentions, as soon as I hit Stapleton Road, I could hear the drugs calling me. I was overwhelmed at the thought of getting rid of the withdrawals I was still experiencing: shivers, aches, lethargy, and disorientation. There was too much temptation around me and I was too weak willed.

Countless times I battled through the sickness of withdrawals with determination but I just could not break free. I could endure the pain, but I couldn't stay clean. Life continued to spiral as we continued in the madness. Anything I could sell went! I remember rummaging through the drawers, desperate to find something to sell, and stumbled on a Bible that had been Andy's. For some reason, I had kept it. As I held it, I remembered Andy and, reminiscing for a moment, I knew I could not get rid of it. Unable to throw it away, I put it back and shut the drawer.

Unfortunately, I caught impetigo and was laid off work whilst working for Dexter. I started withdrawing after a big smoke out. I was a crumpled-up heap of a mess. It had been nearly twenty-four hours since our last hit. I was really sick, sprawled out in bed, tossing, turning, sweating, weak and in pain, when there was a knock at the door. Jake shook me to wake me up; we were being careful about opening the door as we owed money and were avoiding certain people.

Then I got a shock. I heard my little sister's voice.

"Trudy are you in there?" she shouted.

"It's my sister! No way, I don't believe it!" I had not seen Kim for years. What was she doing here at my flat in Bristol? She couldn't see me like this. I had worked so hard to keep my sordid life away from them. I felt so ashamed that I often walked the streets thinking, *They can never know.*

The thought of them seeing me like this was too much to bear. Now, after all this time, here she was at my front door.

"Jake, just leave it," I insisted. "She'll go if you leave it, she can't see me like this."

Kim kept knocking and Jake, being an opportunist, jumped up and headed for the door.

"If you give me a tenner, I'll let you in." Taking the money off her, he shot off out of the door to score.

Kim and her partner came into the bedroom where I lay crumpled up in pain. I was in and out of consciousness. The room consisted of a bed and a wardrobe. I lay on the dishevelled old sweaty sheet that barely covered the mattress.

"Come on, Trudy, we've been trying to get hold of you for ages," she said as she looked down at me with a concern in her eye. She tried to pick me up, but I slumped back down. After picking up the needles and spoons from the mess laid all over the bed, she insisted I come and stay with her. I was too weak to fight, or do anything for that matter – they helped me dress myself and got me into the car to leave.

I stayed a week with her in the kids' bedroom. The first couple of days I kept blacking out and throwing up. My sister called my brother in a panic as they thought I would die. My sister dressed me, bathed me and cleared up my vomit for several days. I reassured her I would be okay, but she was scared and desperate to help. Eventually she managed to get some medication from the doctors to aid me with withdrawal. I didn't dare tell her the mess I was really in and that the medication barely scratched the surface.

My brother kept looking in on me, and we went for a few drinks together when I was over the worst of it. His girlfriend warned me that it would destroy him if I went back to my old ways. I felt bad, but even that was not enough to stop me. I started to get itchy feet – I had been white knuckling it, and although part of me wanted to stay clean, the cravings for drugs were so strong. I insisted on going home, promising that I would not go backwards, but as soon as I landed on Bristol turf I was back on the street corner. I knew it would devastate my brother, but I just had to have a hit. Even though I was lost, and my sister had found me, I could not escape the grip of the drugs on my life.

It was while I was working the streets that I met Annalise. She used to work on the yellow van, which was part of the One25, a charity in Bristol that helped working girls. The van used to circulate the red-light areas offering support. They gave out condoms, cigarettes, and sandwiches. In the winter they gave a hot drink and gloves, and what's more they always seemed to come around at the right time. I would hop on and hop off, relieved to be given some free condoms and often a smoke of a cigarette that would hit the spot just when I needed it.

Annalise was tall, rather lanky in her appearance, and wore gold rimmed glasses that covered those warm eyes on her slender face. She definitely had a fashion sense that was unique to her, often sporting a woolly hat and an array of purple clothing always enhanced by her trainers. She always wore a smile and had a big warm heart. Her encouragement and kindness towards me meant she was never judgemental, and I recognised she carried a quiet authority about her. She knew how to demonstrate tough love. I soon discovered that she was a nun at the Loaves and Fishes Project in St Paul's. She once managed to get me into Dean Crescent, a women's hostel. I stayed a few weeks and started a detox but could not stay off the gear or away from the crack houses, so it fell apart within a month. When I moved to St Paul's, from time to time, if I needed new clothes or a shower, I often used the One25's drop-in centre. They provided a number of services and you could get all kinds of tests done there, but I was never stable enough to make an appointment.

Jake also had a room in a hostel from time to time. Sometimes I could use it to crash out when I didn't have one myself. It was while he was there that I went out to work and nearly had my throat slit by a punter. It was that hostel I made my way back to, broken and defeated, having been dumped out of the car on the industrial estate. It was there that I had my reality check, catching sight of my face in the mirror and realising just how far I had fallen.

Charities like One25 exist for a reason. The streets were dangerous; you had to be able to handle yourself. For me, carrying a knife was too dangerous, I knew how easy it would be to use it. Rather than carry a knife, I thought a snooker ball in a sock would do when I felt threatened. I soon learned I needed to be better equipped, as the threats became more serious. One night I was working the bottom end of Fishponds, and a guy pulled up on my corner to pick me up. I was not tooled up that day.

"Hey, over here," he called over to me. He seemed fine at first. As I walked closer, I could see he was not a usual punter. "Jump in, come on," he said, trying to get me into the car.

He was smiling and offering me a smoke at the same time. He knew I was out for drugs. I did not want to travel and he was giving me a really bad vibe. I could see straight away that he was the volatile type and was high. I knew he was a dangerous person to get stuck with and I needed to get as far away as I could, as quickly as possible.

I declined his invitation and went to walk away, but he jumped out of the car and took some nunchucks out of the boot. He grabbed hold of me and forced me to look into the boot of the car, where he had a big iron bar. He threatened to smash my head in. His overpowering strength holding my twisted arm forced me to get into the car. As he walked round, I thought I could run but feared I would not get away. As he started driving, I figured the only way out was to jump from the car as he was driving. He sped off and I looked for an opportunity to open the door and jump. As we were travelling by St George's Park, the car slowed right down and I grabbed the door where I could see people, jumped out and ran and ran. I already knew of a girl beaten to death in Eastwood. I always wondered about this guy. I had a lucky escape!

Most times on the street it was alright – you'd always get the cheap ones that would try and lure you on the promise of money when they had nothing, but that was par for the course. However, some would try to get something for nothing in other ways. I was working on Fishponds Road when a young guy pulled a knife on me on a street corner and tried to push me into an alley close by.

"Do you know who my bloke is?" I shouted up in his face as I stepped up to him. I was bluffing, but he didn't know that. I made out that my man was some big-time pimp and said he was not far away, and he fell for it. He was obviously inexperienced, as he just let me go. I picked up pace and made sure I got out of sight.

Some nights I was acutely aware of another level of unseen darkness on the streets and an eerie sense of the presence of evil. I had many tight spots with punters: I would get stranded or held hostage, but most of the time, I got what I wanted and made my way out in one piece. Some were as addicted to me and their need to rescue me as I was to drugs. I leaned more on them, as I had my addiction, too. Crack had ravished me. Jake and I seemed to stoop lower and lower. We had let the wrong people into our space, and that meant it added an extra dynamic of unpredictable violence and control. Being an addict means friendships are rarely real, especially when you know a wrong move could mean a hammer or metal bar over your head.

Of course, it gets a bit harder to protect yourself when you have nowhere to go. That was soon to become our reality: the threat of eviction that hung over our heads was about to become more than a threat.

Chapter 18: Living on the Streets

My relationship with Jake was in tatters. My heart had been broken and even though I had behaved selfishly allowing drugs to rule me, I still loved him. It was a very broken love, which was all I had to offer. The violence, jealousy, insecurity and drugs had become such a powerful, destructive force in my life. Eventually, he walked out, and I felt the intense pain of having my heart truly broken. I was tired of everything, and the pain of rejection and losing him was more than I could physically bear.

He did return to the flat for a few weeks before everything went even more wrong. During that time, I was getting desperate to clean up. I went to stay with a punter, Charlie, to help me get clean. Charlie may have been an ex-copper into sadomasochism, but he was kind. The first time I met him on Fox Road, he paid me to hear me talk: he wanted to know about me and my story, why I was working the streets. There were a number of clients that seemed to be lured into this seedy underworld out of a motive of sympathy and curiosity. Yet once they were ensnared that was it, I often felt pity for them, and I likened it to my drug addiction.

"You are too good for this," Charlie insisted. I was sweating, feeling lightheaded and needing a fix. I had been visiting Charlie for a few months. I'd hinted I wanted to get clean and now I was more stressed out with Jake gone, I felt I wanted to change. "Why don't you stay here and I'll help you get off the drugs?" he said.

"I will need some weed, I'll need something."

"That's ok, I can give you some money for that, make sure you get enough to see you through," he insisted.

With the cash he gave me I scored one more time and bought a load of weed to help see me through. I went back, smoked the crack and took a hit; I was happy at least I had some weed left. Now I was somewhat ready – I had gone 'cold turkey' so many times I knew what to expect.

I stayed with him for ten days. The well-known symptoms came again: I was frail and sick, I could not eat, I could barely move off the sofa, so much so that he had to carry me in and out of the bath, prop me up, clothe and take care of me until I was strong enough to be able to do it for myself. I was missing Jake now, though, and as I was feeling better physically my emotions and urges to use were back with a powerful drive. They always played out deceptively. It was always the emotions that came first, but it was as though they were a smoke screen for the real demon calling me.

I decided to head back to my flat to find Jake. I was caught off guard as I arrived at the front door: the place was boarded up, completely secure. I knew this was it. I had been officially evicted; I had no way of getting back in. I couldn't get my hands on anything, my passport, papers, everything was in the flat. Jake had grabbed a few clothes, but that was it. He met me at the house after I called him, and he explained how the bailiffs and security had shown up and given him fifteen minutes to grab some essentials.

I was stunned, with no clue what to do next. I had not seriously thought about being evicted or being made homeless, although it was obvious it had been on the cards. We scored with the money Charlie had given me for some more weed. I never returned and avoided him for several months. I was too consumed with our new situation.

Forty-eight hours had passed, and it was ice cold on the streets. We scored some crack and gear – at least when we took the hit, we were warm for a moment! My legs ached, I was cold to the bone and tired; we would barely sit down to rest and then we'd need to move again. We popped around to our friend Nellie's for a coffee. She had three kids and we stayed as long as we could, but of course soon it was time to go again. Getting comfy and warm only accentuated the pain of having to move on again, the reminder we had nowhere to go.

It was late. The snow was on the ground and seeped through my boots, leaving my toes wet, cold and numb. I headed back down St Mark's Road with Jake and he spotted a car door open. We could not believe our luck. Although it was Baltic in there, somehow it seemed better for an hour or so than roaming the streets.

The following months were tough as we headed into the winter, with snow making the nights freezing. Working and walking the streets all night, not resting or sleeping, led to mental and emotional exhaustion on top of the strain of addiction.

I learned to find shielded shelters for the night: under bridges, doorways, corridors of flats, garages, old damp caravans and squats. Gradually, I took more and more opportunities to stay with punters where I could. I had half a dozen solid regulars that let me use their homes throughout the years I lived on the streets. Staying with them for a couple of days here and there enabled me to get a good bath, catch up on some sleep and eat an actual meal. Some even put me up in hotels or B&Bs. I had always been on the move since I was a teenager. Having that little flat in Bristol for a couple of years was the only time I recall not having to be on the move.

After a bad winter and many months on the street we managed to move in with Toby. He was short, with a skinhead, and was a bit of a traveller. We met him through a mutual friend when he came to score from us. He told us about how he had lived in the valleys in South Wales. I pictured a load of valleys and a little caravan in the middle of nowhere and thought how strange! Toby had no idea what he was letting himself in for. We were in a mess and brought havoc with us. In those days, we took big risks in the way we used our drugs.

It was during the time we were staying at Toby's that I met Daryl. He picked me up on Fishponds Road one morning, gave me fifty pounds for a five-minute chat and dropped me home. I was so relieved he had come along on a Saturday morning when Fishponds Road was usually dead. Daryl called for me a bit later so that I could go and buy some drugs. Daryl was married and had two sons; he had been a church goer but had built up some frustrations around the way he perceived things should be done. He had a good heart and tried to be my saviour. He became a loyal punter and friend; surprisingly, he stuck with me, although he barely got a thing off me bar my company and a load of grief. He brought me money all the time, which fed and enabled my habit, and I was never sure who was more dependent, him or me. I did know that I depended upon his supply of cash and him driving me around gave me respite from walking.

Jake and I stayed with Toby for several months. The house was cold and damp but we were grateful for a room and a roof over our head. He did not mind us staying at first, as he wanted the drugs and he thought we would be the answer to his habit. We were not easy guests, and as we continued to grow worse, the situation intensified. Toby became increasingly agitated as he could not handle us. We took less and less notice of his requests and demands. Our lifestyle meant that we took over the house; it already wasn't great, but now it looked like a rubbish tip, with paraphernalia everywhere. There was always the smell of smoke and the place was full of junkies. We were up morning till night smoking and injecting. It seemed there was always further downhill for us to slip: we still shared spoons with people that were high risk, like Hepatitis C carriers, and we continued to deteriorate. It was a hostile and volatile environment and we fobbed him off over the rent, always promising and never delivering. He ended up leaving as he lost control of the flat and we would not move out.

It was early one morning when I heard a bang, and then a second one. It sounded like a police raid. I ran to Jake, and together we stashed what gear we had, then stood at the top of the stairs. There was no way out of the house. I ran to the window, but there were no police.

"It's not the old bill!" I shouted.

Then I heard someone call through the letterbox: they had come to repossess the house. Realising it was the council, Jake got some wood and used it to wedge the door, which was already strong.

"Squatter's rights!" he shouted.

"Squatter's rights!" I joined in. We both shouted as we ran back up the stairs. As they left, we amused ourselves with our momentary victory. We knew our days there were numbered but we would work at keeping someone present in the place at all times. We were not keen to end up back on the streets.

As time went on, I started to get paranoid about Jake and his fidelity. We had lost all the trust between us. I had recently robbed a girl he knew and he was upset about it. We had a massive fight. I hid behind the sofa, paranoid, listening in on his conversations and trying to catch him out as I thought he may be cheating on me. I wished I hadn't, as he spilled out all his anger and resentment about me and my using. It was another blow to me and to our relationship. Hearing his anger, the feelings of rejection rose up, crushing me. I left and went to stay with a different punter that had come on the scene. The next time I popped back, our squat was boarded up.

So, I was back on the streets. I stayed with different punters where I could, but most of the time me and Jake stuck together: it meant we had each other to lean on. We slept where we could, and when it poured with rain, we got some cardboard and tried to keep dry under an office door. It was futile, really. Wet, cold weather was always the worst enemy when you had no supplies. Everywhere we stayed was damp and we needed each other's body heat to keep warm. We were back to staying in different squats, old shops, derelict buildings anywhere we could find. As we continued in the madness of living on the streets, there were some close shaves.

One time, we were staying in an old shop that was a complete hazard to get in and out of. One afternoon I had been out to work, and on my way back to meet Jake to score, we saw the place was on fire. We realised we must have left a candle burning, so that was the end of that squat.

We moved into an old nursing home that had been burned out: it was a complete mess, full of asbestos and with no windows, but it was a shelter. There were dozens of rooms although they were wrecked and of course uninhabitable. I had just come back from scoring when there was a fire. The whole place was full of things that were flammable, and the fire spread quickly. Soon, the whole building ignited. I was on the pipe taking a hit at the time.

"We need to get out of here!" Jake yelled. "The place is going to blow!"

"One minute!" I shouted. All that was going through my mind was one more lick on the pipe: I took another, then another. Jake charged round the corner as I desperately inhaled the last of the fumes.

"What the hell are you doing? We need to move now!" I could see he was panicking but I didn't care, I just needed another lick first. Looking back, I was fearless. I had become so desensitised to risk that it was only extreme pain or shock that got my attention. Thankfully the fire was put out and the place did not crumble to the ground.

We ended up staying there a long time, but we were now limited to a single room with no windows on the edge of the building.

"Come on!" Jake would say, trying to entice me to go and get some food. He had discovered places we could go to get a meal. I calculated how much time it would take to get there and back: easily an hour and a half. *Is he mad? Why would I waste my time*? I could have secured a client in the time it took him to do that trip. It was a no brainer. Jake seldom got to bring something back. Over the years, though, he was the one that landed the occasional hostel or room for a while, and even though they were strict on rules about overnight guests he managed to sneak me in unseen. The hostels never lasted long.

I was always too chaotic to find anywhere. I never saw getting a room or a place as a priority, which meant sticking to the streets, punters, or crack houses. I didn't have the time, energy or mental capacity to see through what I needed to do. I was always chaotic, restless and anxious, driven by my relentless need for drugs and money. I had an insatiable appetite that could never be quenched.

Chapter 19: Obsessed

I was only ever moving in one direction: to fuel the god of addiction in my life. Nothing else mattered or warranted my energy or focus. Jake and I often separated for spells due to the increasing violence and chaos between us. During a separation period, I miraculously managed to get a bedsit through a drugs worker trying to get me into rehab. I succeeded in keeping the room for about eight weeks whilst waiting for funding for the rehab, thanks to punters who paid my rent. I needed to have the stability of an address in order to get into the rehab. I spent weeks at a time without sleep: paranoid, hallucinating, and fitting. I would sit in the room, smoking crack with my ear to the door, completely paranoid, or scratching around on the floor for crack for hours. It was common behaviour after smoking crack; I would pick anything up and try to smoke it, till it hit my lungs and the vile smell of singed hair or plastic I had attempted to smoke choked me.

Once I barricaded myself in for two full weeks, not letting anyone in or out, only emerging to score. I would wake up with no recollection of what had happened after I arrived back at the bedsit. Too often, I'd wake up in the communal kitchen with crack cocaine scattered all over the floor and under the table, having blacked out after being up so long and smoking so much. My memory would always be fuzzy, so I'd scramble around, looking for my drugs. Too many times, I'd start convulsing uncontrollably – one particular time I got trapped in a doorway whilst convulsing, unable to stop while my head banged from side to side of the door frame.

It was Daryl, one of my faithful punters, who agreed to take me to the rehab interview at Broadway Lodge. He was desperate for me to go in. He beeped the horn and rang my phone to let me know he was outside. I came down, having just finished taking a hit. I told him that I wasn't going anywhere without scoring first; I needed a pipe. I had him drive round to make sure I could get some crack and smack. I was convinced I could do nothing without a hit in me. He was getting nervous and tried to get firm with me; I never saw him that angry and frustrated.

"You got what you need, now let's go," he demanded. I smoked my crack on the pipe and made do with chasing some gear on the foil all the way down in the car. We were cutting it fine, eventually arriving at the rehab. On arrival I wandered up to the receptionist, and thankfully they were still in an interview so that gave me time. The receptionist told me to take a seat. It was a small area, clean and well kept, but there was one thing on my mind. *There's time for another pipe!*

"Have you got a toilet?"

"Yes, just there!"

The toilet was to the left of the receptionist. It was obvious that it was risky – it was right next to her. I went into the toilet and hastily smoked a few draws on my cigarette to create the ash I needed. Pulling out my pipe, I placed a piece of crack on and took another couple of blasts. I wasn't oblivious to the smell, but the addict in me put the drug first. As I came out, they called me into the interview room. Later they showed me around the building before asking me to wait whilst they discussed my case. I was asked to sit outside if I wanted to smoke. In the front garden I sat down and, with the pipe in my jacket, I attempted to slyly tuck my head into the jacket as I loaded the pipe. I took one hit, two hits, and then some of the guys came round the corner, obviously on their house duties. One of the guys looked surprised.

"Hey, you can't do that here!" he insisted. I knew it was wrong and inconsiderate, but I wasn't bothered that I was overstepping the mark smoking in a rehab. I knew that was my cue to get out of there to score some more gear.

I was offered a place at the Broadway Lodge rehab, where they ran a twelve-step program. Even though I was granted the funding, I ended up running after six weeks, being triggered by weight gain and shoplifting after a day out. The staff did their best to talk me round to staying, and I knew they were right, but my drive to use and to leave had taken over.

I landed back on the streets in Bristol, back with Jake again as I had nowhere else to go. By now we were staying in a rundown old shop that was not being used. It was still full of junk that we tripped over, walking past mirrors, chairs, draws and other random stuff piled up. It was cold, wet, and dingy due to broken windows, but the barrage of stuff helped insulate us. We could barely squeeze in and up the stairs, but it was a shelter.

It was a Saturday night when I left there after taking our last hit and walked down to Fishponds Road. My plan was to get a minimum of fifty pounds from the next guy, although if I could make a hundred that would do me for now. All I needed to go back to the squat was heroin so that we had some to wake up to.

I left in a short black skirt, heels, and a little fur coat. I picked up a punter straight away. Then I saw Jinx, Riley and Mix, a few other working girls – they were heading over to get some crack, and the temptation was too much. I decided I would catch a lift over too and score, then I would come back. I scored some heroin and crack but not from my usual dealer. I ended up round at Snoop's; he had people round and we smoked crack all night. I was exhausted and kept going till I was forced to crash out. When I woke up, I took the needle to hit up and nothing happened. I shot the rest up to get it straight into my nervous system, but still nothing: the gear was duff. Had someone messed with it while I was asleep? Had I been scammed? I couldn't believe it! This was the first time I had ever had gear that didn't work at all. Snoop was up, but he had no heroin, he was more into smoking crack.

"Come on, come with me," he said.

I didn't want to move. I was sick from not having any heroin for over sixteen hours. Jake was due to be paid, but I would have to walk to him and I could barely move. What was more, I knew I would have to pacify him as he had expected me back Saturday night, and it was now Monday morning. Snoop wanted to go to the Loaves and Fishes Project to get some food and wouldn't leave me.

"Come on!" he shouted, insisting I went with him. He wasn't prepared to leave me alone in the house, probably worried I would rob the little he had. I dragged myself up, feeling weak and breathless, breaking out in cold sweats as we walked along the road. It was only around the corner but it felt like miles.

We arrived at the project and I collapsed on the doorstep. I already had a severe chest infection and could barely breathe. I was five and a half stone, sick and weak. Snoop got his usual food supply from the nuns and left me with them, as they insisted on taking me in. They lifted me and walked me in, placing me on the sofa and covering me with a warm blanket, which brought a bit of comfort for a while.

The nuns who worked at the Loaves and Fishes Project gave out parcels of dry food to those who found themselves in challenging circumstances. I had picked stuff up there occasionally. Annalise lived at the project in St Paul's with Sue and Rosie. All three were kind and warm.

Sue brought me a hot drink. I lay there with a blanket over me, shivering. The noises of a full house were becoming more muffled as I started to drift in and out of consciousness; my chest was rattling and I could barely breathe. Annalise suggested I see a doctor. I just wanted to score. We didn't have phones at the time, as we'd sold them. I knew there was no way I could make it the few miles to where Jake would be. Using the phone at the nuns, I tried calling some punters, but no one was answering, everyone seemed to be out of town. This never happened. *Why now?*

Annalise started to talk to me about getting help. The nuns were discussing me in the other room. Annalise had remembered a Christian rehab she had information about in South Wales. I went along with the idea, as they were being so kind and I was too weak to argue. I knew she was talking sense, but I was not really interested.

The only thing on my mind was holding out for a punter but time was ticking away. A doctor they knew prescribed me antibiotics. They spoke to someone in the rehab in South Wales, called Victory Outreach, who then faxed through an application form. Even as Annalise was filling it in, I knew as soon as I could get through to someone I would be gone, but so far though the only promise I had was after ten that night. *Where is Daryl when I need him?* By now it was early evening and I had submitted to the idea of going to rehab. To my surprise they accepted me there and then. I was too weak to argue and found myself on my way to South Wales.

The place was in the back of beyond, and we finally arrived after getting lost. I still wasn't quite sure how I had let them talk me into coming to Wales. No one knew I had gone. I stumbled as I got out of the car; twenty-four hours had passed since I had taken a hit. The three nuns – Rosie, who was four-foot-nothing, and Annalise and Sue who were both quiet and gentle by nature – carried me up a steep hill and into the rehab. They placed me on the sofa with the blanket over me. I was so ill that the staff called the director. Seeing how unwell I was, she suggested they take me to A&E. I insisted that I would be fine, I just needed ice cream and I would manage. I did not want the embarrassment of the hospital knowing that I was just withdrawing. I knew if I put my mind to it, I could work through the withdrawals. I had done it before.

With the help and encouragement of those in the home as well as Kerry, my roommate and buddy, I did it. I was violently sick and suffered bad diarrhoea for nearly a week but managed to get through it. I just remember thinking: *where on Earth am I?*

When I was ill, they prayed for me. After their working day, they would watch the news and drink tea. I wondered what planet I was on. I had been used to going two hundred miles an hour. What was more, they played actual tambourines! I had never seen anything like it! At the time, I was just glad it wasn't me.

After a couple of weeks, I was getting stronger and feeling motivated towards change. The director decided to move me to another one of their rehab homes called the Barley Mow in Birmingham. I suspect there were too many new girls together and they decided I would be the best one to move.

I liked it there. It was a small house, quite different to the one in Wales. It was not as isolated, and we were allowed out, so we went to the job centre to sort my money out. I saw a girl I knew from Broadway Lodge, a former rehab. She slipped me her number. I got home and I could not stop thinking about seeing her. I knew I was in the right place and I had been feeling stronger, but I just gave into the temptation and left to meet her for a smoke. I organised for a punter to drive to Birmingham to collect me. Interestingly, I always knew that I had left something spiritual behind, but at the time I didn't know what it was. I was conscious that I was more than flesh and bones and that something I could not name or identify was going on inside of me.

In total, I had tried getting clean and detoxing thirty-three times. Every time I picked up again it was worse, I fell harder and faster. With each failed attempt, hope was slipping away.

Returning back to Bristol, I stayed at my punter's house and went out to score. I got heroin that I was told was 'good gear' and took the hit. I suddenly woke up damp from sweat and laid out on a cold floor. My head was spinning; my whole body seemed to be paralysed. Feeling disorientated, it took me a while even to figure out where I was. It was as though my memory had been completely wiped. I had no idea how long I had been there for. I must have been there for ages. I looked to my side, seeing the spoon and needle, and figured it had been hours. *Why did no one come to look for me?* I didn't even recall going to the bathroom. I stumbled to my feet and made my way downstairs gasping for air. I'd obviously overdosed – I had heard the gear here was strong. I got out of there knowing that I was fortunate to still be alive.

Jake was still in the burned-out old nursing home. I was pretty much doing what I wanted and taking care of myself. I rang to meet up with Jake. We were not together as much now – he was a mess, and I was staying here and there with punters. I scored some crack and heroin and made it back to see Jake at the old nursing home to share a smoke with him. It grew dark early, as we were heading into the autumn, which was not good for smoking as there were no candles, in fact no light anywhere to see what I was doing. I didn't have my glass pipe, so we had to use a can for the crack.

Jake turned up a bit off key, so we started arguing, as usual. I told him I had a smoke but chose not to declare everything I had; I always held a bit back. I told him to set the pipe up. As I prepared to break the stone to put on the pipe, he randomly hit the stone I held right out of my hand and it fell to the floor. The room was almost pitch black with scarcely any light. As he came close to knock it out of my hand, I could smell the drink on him. He accused me of being unfaithful and sly. I had to admit sly wasn't untrue, but I was not unfaithful. I had at least come to smoke with him. Then he got angry because we couldn't see the crack. I took another stone, we took a hit each and then I started looking for the first stone. I was so mad at him.

"What are you doing?" I shouted at him.

The next thing I felt was a blow to my face. My nose cracked and my tooth went right through my lip. All I could think to do was hit back. He grabbed me, punched me harder and shoved me to the floor. I fell and hit my head, cracking it open on an old metal bed frame that was in the room. Blood spattered onto the floor as I steadied myself – I was definitely concussed.

I tried to stagger out of the room, but Jake came after me, and we became a tangle of punches and kicks yet again. Dizziness and nausea came over me as we wrestled one another to the floor; he rolled over on top of me and held me to the floor with his body weight. He put his hands tight around my neck, squeezing and squeezing. I couldn't breathe. Thankfully, someone walked past. He released my throat and stormed off.

I managed to get to my feet. It was all I could do to stumble my way to Maria's place, a working girl who I had met on the street. She took me to her place on Ashley Hill – to this day, I don't know how I made it. When we got there, I just collapsed. She cleaned me up, although I probably should have had stitches. I was in bed for three days straight, unable to move. She supplied me with gear, but I knew I could not stay, and it was my turn to make some money. Although I was still fragile, I left and never went back. I went back to the streets, crashing at a local punter's place and avoiding Jake entirely. Our relationship was now broken beyond repair.

Chapter 20: Busted

I had made idols of crack and heroin and worshiped them from morning till night: they received all my devotion, attention, affection and energy, and in return they had completely destroyed me. Having failed so many times to get clean, I had lost all hope that I could change. The hope of a better future had been completely obliterated.

Jake and I were finished for good; there was no going back. Too much had happened, and we both carried so much unresolved hurt, anger and bitterness that staying in each other's company was dangerously volatile. I took up the offer of staying with a regular punter who helped to keep me in a supply of drugs. Another of my regular punters had got wind that I was no longer with Jake and brought me a lot of nice expensive clothes and shoes. He thought now Jake was off the scene, I may take him up on his offer of getting married, which I would never take seriously, even if he ever really meant it.

Feeling good and all dressed up in some fancy clothes, I was itching to get out and make some money. With a bit of cash I had from my punter, I called Lyrics, a DJ that I'd seen earlier in the day, and met up with him and a few others. We had a bit of a bingeing session on crack. Once it was all gone, we mustered enough between us to score again. We visited Lyrics' mate AJ, his old-time friend who was a Rastafarian. We'd seen each other before but this was the first time I'd properly met him. He was not a street dealer, more underground and off road, which made him more successful at it.

AJ lived in a block of flats that had good secure gates, which proved useful to keep most people out. We made our way up the stairs to the top flat and knocked on the door.

"Hey AJ, what's up?" Lyrics asked.

"I'm good man, long time no see. Come in." I didn't seem to need an immediate introduction.

"Got any white?" Lyrics asked. The table was set up with the pipe and foil with AJ's gear on. We scored. It was good stuff and a good size considering we were in St Paul's. After a few blasts, Lyrics decided we should hit the road.

AJ seemed to hold himself together well for someone who smoked crack and was fairly quiet. He had an air of mystery and intrigue about him, and he made sure I knew I was invited anytime to score. I liked him; he seemed a different breed to most of the guys on the street, a bit more laid back and safer to be around. Later that night I scored some crack from him, and we spent the night and early hours smoking and talking. We soon began a casual relationship that went on to become more committed, and it brought the added advantage of a new roof over my head.

Life was a little easier there: I got more drugs for free, and living in St Paul's at AJ's was convenient, giving me quick access to the streets and even more drugs. The streets in St Paul's were not the same as in Easton. I had to watch my back more – it was 'dog eat dog', as they say – but I knew it was the drugs that made people like this. Somewhere deep inside me lived a kindness that always sought to see the potential in people, even though I was a mess.

Most of my days were spent roaming crack houses, telephone boxes or in doorways, smoking crack and hitting up. Robbing the people I smoked with was a priority focus, and if I did not try and rob them, they would try and get one over on me. Friendships were often a facade with double motives.

I was at another user's place one day, a guy called Wylie who also lived in St Paul's. His flat had become a major crack den, and I went to see if there was an opportunity to slip a few crack stones off the side as the crack cocaine was being cut up. That's how it was there, of course, those cutting up were aware of the usual likely suspects with the same intentions as mine. Having to watch them all like a hawk, I knew an opportunity would soon arise if I stuck close by. I edged myself closer, slipped a stone and went into the other room to quickly smoke it off. Just as I took the last blast: Bang! Bang!

"Get down on the floor now!"

Panicking, I jumped behind the door and pulled the handle towards me. The armed response and drugs squad were there arresting everyone; they had managed to get the stash, the scales and some cash. One by one, the police removed everyone from the room, then the police left too. They had taken about twenty people out of the place. I could still hear the radios and a couple of officers left. One suddenly came back into the room and hesitated at the door. My heart was pounding, gripped by fear.

He left. I stood frozen behind that door. Then I heard footsteps coming back again. I breathed in and squeezed myself into the corner. I wasn't sure if someone had snitched, or if it was the officer's instinct, but he pulled the door away.

"What have we got here then? Come on."

It was all over, but getting locked up that night was more of an inconvenience than anything else.

The activity around AJ and I continued to increase. Dealing meant the flat became more busy and more hazardous. I still worked the credit cards where I could. I preferred them because I'd become accustomed to adopting false identities. It was preferable to working the streets.

One Saturday morning, after a late night, I woke up feeling really sick. We had gone to bed with barely enough gear in us to keep us well. I had woken up with that restlessness, with the worry of money and the desire to get a hit running riot through me. AJ was still asleep, but I lay there sweating. I knew he had twenty pounds saved for this morning's fix.

Greed started to consume me. I convinced myself that I could score and get a punter, fix up, get some crack and put the money back before he woke up. It was unrealistic, but the impulse was so strong that I jumped up. I knew I was betraying him, but the guilt was not enough to deter me. I crept out of the bed, tiptoed over to his jeans and slyly slipped the note out of his pocket. I glanced over at him whilst he was asleep and slipped out of the door to score.

I always found St Paul's a harder place to pick up on the streets at certain times, especially at eight on a Saturday morning. The road was like a ghost town. I scored, but I was on edge, smoking and wondering if AJ had woken up yet. After nine, the streets were still dead. I could not face going back yet, and then when I did get a punter, I just wanted another smoke. I knew it was too late to return to AJ; by now, he would have discovered me and the money gone, so I went AWOL for days to avoid going back. He got wind that I was floating around crack houses. When eventually I did find myself forced to come back, he was raging. I had never seen him lose his temper. He caught me outside the back door and beat me. When things like that happen, a little bit more respect is lost and things always change for the worse.

AJ had a Bible in the house and was God-conscious. He considered himself more of a Rasta, but although that made up part of his understanding of God, he did not follow their traditions. Yet often I saw a gentle humble man with a glimmer of something good in him. I remember being drawn to his little leather-backed Bible, and picking it up and reading it. At the time, I felt like God was speaking to me. I don't remember what I read, but I was impacted by it and started rambling.

However, there were also times I was acutely aware of a looming sense of evil in the house. I was acquainted with the fact he had dabbled in a bit of traditional witchcraft and had shown me some of the items stored in his cupboard. One time after a row, he even screamed at me, "You're the devil!" The way he shouted at me it seemed like he believed I really was!

Things seemed to be getting a whole lot darker around us, and more sordid in so many ways, with betrayal on both parts. I didn't care too much; I was out most of the time, caught up in my own addiction and controlled by my self-absorbed nature. On occasion, the depth of sorrow and pain would overwhelm me and it became increasingly difficult to run from. Everything that was suppressed deep inside was overtaking me and I could not stop the feelings of deep despair.

AJ and I had been busted so many times, the place had become red hot. After a heavy session that had been non-stop for days, we finally slept, but not for long: the door was being broken down with the familiar sound of a battering ram. I had to move quickly. I was so sick but I didn't want to get nicked – I was already in breach of my bail. I jumped up and dived out the window onto the roof, even though I hated heights. I hid down on the roof where there was a narrow ledge facing some businesses in Portland Square. Shortly after, the police helicopter hovered overhead.

"You are surrounded, come down off the roof."

The helicopter continued to circle, the megaphone blaring commands at me. I knew there was no way I could get down except to go back the way I came. I sat for a while ignoring them and eventually a copper opened the window to come out to me. I climbed back through the window bedraggled, and the officer grabbed my arm, twisting it behind my back to put the handcuffs on.

I was remanded again. After several weeks of being locked up, my solicitor managed to get me out on a Drug Treatment and Testing Order and a tag whilst awaiting sentence for Possession with Intent to Supply. I was facing those charges as a result of us being busted a couple of months before.

Thanks to AJ's ability to deal, our habits had escalated to another level. We were ripping our way through wild amounts of crack and it was only a matter of time before we got busted yet again. We knew it would happen, we were just waiting for them, but still the element of surprise can leave you unprepared. As soon as I heard the familiar sound of the door being rammed in, I hid the first ounce where I thought they'd never find it. I grabbed another and tried to get that out of sight too, but as they moved us around to search it fell to the floor. Everyone was marched into the lounge; the room was heaving with other people who had scored from us. As the police continued with their search, all they had was paraphernalia: needles, spoons, crack pipes, foils and every other thing that pointed to the use of drugs. They found a few credit cards that no one would own up to; it could have been anyone in the flat with the number of questionable characters there.

When they finished tearing the place apart, they arrested me and took me to the station. I was interviewed several times. They were desperate to catch us in the act of dealing. It was AJ they really wanted, but they only had a couple of small ten-pound bags. The rest was a lump, which I said was personal. Without my confession or concrete evidence, a possession charge was the best they could put together. They kept me as long as they could, but in the end they let me go on bail while the gear was tested. They added a curfew to my tag as part of my bail condition, but it was too much for me to handle. I was meant to be confined from seven at night till seven in the morning. I couldn't keep to it. I cut the tag off and left it in the flat. I decided I would take my chances.

Things continued to escalate out of control. My relationship with AJ was increasingly strained. Eventually, the usual damage came with the addiction: mistrust, betrayal, selfishness and greed got the better of us. We had been busted many times and he was on eviction notice. Things were chaotic and out of control in the flat, with too many devious and dangerously unpredictable characters coming and going. I started to avoid going back: I didn't like the vibes and felt unsettled when I was there, as though I needed to continually watch over my shoulder.

Chapter 21: Victory Outreach

The one good thing in my life at the time was Tiger, a little white westie. We had got him and his sister from Kitty, another acquaintance. She had brought these pure breeds on a dodgy chequebook. She came into the flat high.

"This is Crack and Smack," she said, introducing us to the two tiny puppies, who peered out of the top of her handbag. We ended up keeping one and renaming him Tiger because of his bold personality. Inevitably he too acquired an increasing appetite for crack, as his curious nose had become a regular hoover in our flat. This little dog softened my heart and enabled me to feel again. I loved him so much and he loved and depended on me. I didn't care that he ate my high heels and anything else he could get his teeth into. I finally genuinely cared about something that was not drugs. He helped soften and prepare my heart for what was about to come.

One afternoon, I called into the nuns as we were skint and I wanted to get some electric and food. I was a wreck, my usual self: starving, sketchy and highly strung. I chaotically smoked one cigarette after the other in a frenzy and in some vain attempt to try and calm myself down after a session on crack. The conversation began again about me getting some help. Annalise had never failed to encourage and challenge me over the years. She could see I was in a really bad way and only getting worse.

"Why don't you go back to Victory Outreach? I am sure I still have their number." I knew she was worried about me.

"I can't. What about Tiger?" He was my biggest excuse. I was not going to leave him. I had grown too attached to him and was never going to leave him in the flat.

The biggest obstacle I had to overcome was taking that active step of change. I didn't have anything to lose, but it was anxiety and that fear of the unknown that held me back. Although I had taken the steps before, it never stopped the panic that came with it. Mulling it over, I decided I would go. AJ agreed it was the best thing, as we were about to be evicted.

The day I was due to leave, I freaked: I was enjoying the drugs too much to leave. My head was in a spin; I wanted another hit. The knock at the door sent panic through me. *Not today, not now*, I thought. They knocked on the door again, and I made AJ answer it. They came in and I hid in the wardrobe. I could hear them asking to look around, as though they did not believe I was not there. I heard their footsteps in the corridor and the door shut behind them. AJ was not impressed having to lie to them, especially as they were nuns.

Not long after that day, I called in to see the nuns again. I was gaunt and skinny. My face was sunken, my eyes wide; I was white as a ghost. I was really low, feeling completely hopeless. I kept masking it with drugs, but I was dying on the inside. All the pain, immense sadness and brokenness was catching up with me. I had not stopped to consider how my actions had led me to this place, but the hurt was so overwhelming that I could no longer fob off those feelings or escape from them.

There was a volunteer there called Gill, silently working away at the large dining table, who had started to volunteer for the nuns after becoming a widow and retiring. She was tall and slim, with the demeanour of a contented soul – she looked a bit like a librarian! Every time I saw her, she displayed a gentle and calming manner. She had heard of my plight and she agreed to look after Tiger for me while I got help. It was no small thing, because he too needed rehabilitating.

So, it was agreed. I felt this was a good arrangement and I was happy for Tiger to be with Gill, who eventually kept him as a life companion. She later told me it took years to rehabilitate him!

The nuns came again to collect me. I was too sick to move and not ready to leave, shivering from withdrawals under the old blanket while we waited for some gear. Annalise made her way into the room after AJ had reluctantly let her into see me.

"Trudy, is that you?" I recognised the familiar sound of her authoritative voice. I was too weak and tired to speak, so I put my hand out from beneath the blanket to let her know I was there. She came closer and put my hand in hers.

"Trudy you really need to come. This is the last opportunity you have with Victory Outreach. Are you still wanting to go?"

I squeezed her hand to indicate I wanted to go.

"Right, I will be back at three to collect you. This is it, Trudy, it's your last chance. You need to have your bags packed and be ready, as I can't wait around."

I knew this was it. AJ scored and was keen to see me go. We'd been talking about it all week, as he was due to be evicted any day. Annalise picked me up with my belongings at half past three. I had already packed, knowing the day was potentially coming.

We went to the Loaves and Fishes Project where she lived to collect a few things. I had been trying to score some hash or weed to take with me to help me with the rattle, but I'd run out of time and they were not willing to let me go off on my own. I had about two spliffs on me and that was it. I wasn't sure how I was going to get through cold turkey. My plan was to stay three months and return. I thought that should be long enough; I could not face the idea of a year or more.

When we arrived in Wales, I was strip-searched in the bathroom. All my things were piled up outside the door whilst the support worker went through them. This time I had walked in with about three large suitcases and bags of clothes. I remember someone commenting that they'd never seen so many pairs of jeans!

I was surprised but glad they had been willing to take me whilst I was still on bail, and I was due to surrender at the station in Bristol in a few weeks. They had managed to get me a detox from the doctors, though it was barely enough to scratch the sides, but to my mind something was better than nothing. I still had to sweat it out. I knew the score: after week one it would not be so bad, after a month I should get some partial sleep. I had some blood tests taken and the results showed I had Hepatitis C.

It was in the few weeks following that I struggled with my emotions, wanting drugs. AJ and the dog played on my mind too, but again they were a smoke screen, because deep down I wanted to use. I was restless, unwell and distracted.

I shared a room with two girls, Carole and Lucy. Carole used to read to me from the Bible – most of it went over my head, but I liked her. She was Scottish, in her late thirties, old school but with a great sense of humour. I did not recognise Lucy at first, but she recognised me: apparently, she'd scored from us. She had a sweet-looking, fresh face that appeared innocent; she was a warm hearted, gentle character. I loved sharing a room with them both. I couldn't recall laughing clean belly laughter like I did with them for years. It was really refreshing.

While there, Carole gave me a tiny little promise book that had some sayings from the Bible in it. As I hastily made my way through the little booklet, these words caught my attention:

> *"Come to me, all you who are weary and burdened, and I will give you rest. Take my yoke upon you and learn from me, for I am gentle and humble in heart, and you will find rest for your souls. For my yoke is easy and my burden is light." Jesus.* (Matthew 11:28-30)

The words hit me at my core and spoke directly to me about my situation. I felt weary and exhausted, as though I had the world on my shoulders. Life had worn me down from years of addiction, abuse and emotional trauma. Those words were personal and found a landing strip. They connected with my heart and stuck with me.

In those few weeks I was in Victory Outreach, I was taken to a Christian meeting in St David's Hall in Cardiff. As I walked in, I was blown away at the size of the place, how posh it looked with its high ceilings and expensive red plush carpet. We travelled up the escalators, passing by other theatre spaces, and entered the auditorium. There was a real buzz about the place: it was packed, with seating capacity for up to two thousand people. We were seated in the upper seating area.

I was stimulated and excited by seeing so many people. I'd never attended such an event. There was excitement amongst the girls because the guys from the men's rehab were also there. Most of the time they were kept apart, for obvious reasons, but today I was more interested in soaking up this new experience. I was completely oblivious to the fact that we were about to hear an internationally renowned man of God speak to us. I just sat there, taking in the thrilling atmosphere and loving the freedom of being out of the rehab home.

The band began to play and all over the room people sang. I didn't know the songs, but I enjoyed having an opportunity to have a bit of a dance, lost in the moment and unaware that I was the only one swinging my hips and raising my arms without a care. Then I realised everyone else in the home seemed a little stiff in comparison, and they were amused with watching me. I was so fresh into rehab and unaware of my behaviour, which was obvious, but I carried on regardless of any glances.

Sometime after, a man came up onto the stage. he was introduced as the Evangelist Reinhard Bonnke. There was a huge screen behind him, which enabled us to see him up close. He wore a dark coloured suit and a kind smile, and he had a sparkle in his eyes; they glistened with joy when he spoke. He spoke with a strong German accent, yet he spoke so clearly and passionately, and his voice held a warm authority, such as I had never heard before. His voice thundered across St David's Hall, and I was captivated, listening intently with my eyes fixed on him.

I do not remember much of what he said, as my ability to concentrate was so poor. It was when I heard him say Jesus died for my sins, I knew I was a sinner. He continued to talk about my need for a saviour. He told us:

> *Jesus loves you and He died on the cross for you. He died in your place so that you could be free. If you were the only person alive, He would still have died for you. For God so loved the world that He gave His only begotten son that whosoever would believe in Him would have everlasting life, for He did not send His son into the world to condemn the world but that the world through Him might be saved.*

I felt my heart being pricked and as he continued to speak about what Jesus had done to restore me into a relationship with God, I felt a warmth well up inside. No one had ever died for me before. Then he said that whoever wanted to receive God's forgiveness in their life and have a fresh start could do so by receiving the free gift of salvation in and through God's son, Jesus. He started to pray and asked people to follow him in a prayer to receive Jesus. With his powerful voice, this humble yet gifted man said that whoever wanted to be filled with the Holy Spirit and His power should come to the front.

I sat there for a moment, thinking to myself. *What was the Holy Spirit?* I watched as people began to leave their seats. I did not fully understand all that he said, but I felt an urge to run down to the front. We were seated high up in the auditorium, but one of the ladies from the rehab had been watching me. She leaned over and asked me if I wanted to go down. I had a strong desire to go. We made our way down, and with the crowd heaving, I pushed my way through. I could hear the Evangelist making his way through the crowd. I could not see him and tried on tiptoe to see where he was.

The lighting was dim, and there was a warmth and a closeness that pervaded the atmosphere as the people squashed together. There was what felt like a thick weighty cloud over us. I felt that God was close; I never sensed such expectancy and power. The atmosphere was super charged and increasing as my expectation increased. Then suddenly, I felt a hand rest on my head and a heat and an energy surged through me as I was prayed for in the name of Jesus.

Then the Evangelist asked for all those who had responded to this invitation to receive Jesus to come to one side, and we were ushered into a room and given some material to read through. My head was spinning. I seemed to float along, feeling as though there was some blanket warming me that felt thick but comforting. Coming out, I felt somewhat dazed but different. We left not long after and travelled back to the home. I was deeply affected by all that had happened, but my head and my emotions were still very much running wild.

Chapter 22: Locked Up

Three weeks had passed since I arrived at the rehab, and it had been less than a week since I'd said that prayer. I was due to go back and sign on at the police station to answer my bail. The house manager drove me down to the police station in Bristol, where I signed on. While we were there, I tried to convince her to let me visit Social Security to chase my dole money. She reassured me we would contact them when we got home. As she drove us back to Wales, I was feeling restless and on edge. When I got back, I discovered I had received a backdated cheque from the social: after paying my rent, I was left with about four hundred and fifty pounds. I thought I had hit the jackpot! I refused the house manager's offer to lock the money away. I could feel it burning a hole in my pocket as I started to think about scoring.

I started to pace the house. Having that much money was too much of a temptation. I felt the impulse to leave, but I knew I was on bail. I decided I would go and score and return to the rehab in a few days. My desire overtook all sense. My only other dilemma was how would I get out of the house: I couldn't get out the back door as people were in the kitchen, and I'd never get away out of the front door without being seen. The house was on a hill and three stories high, but there was a side entrance on the middle landing. The only thing was it was guarded by a hefty basset hound called Barney. I decided to make a run for it anyway. I grabbed a bag and legged it through the corridor, with Barney barking like crazy. Just as I went to jump the gate, he managed to take a bite at my behind – thankfully it was just a nip, but it made me run faster. I got over the gate and ran and ran through the back streets until I reached a pub and called a taxi to get away.

I managed to make it back to Bristol. As I walked in, AJ was pleased to see me and of course I had a wedge. For a moment my heart was warmed by seeing him, and I was pleased to share some good vibes. People started to comment on the difference they could see in me. Even I realised I had stopped swearing, and up until now I struggled to express and articulate myself because my swearing had been so profound for so long. Now I was hearing others swear, it was grating on me, but after a week I slipped right back into swearing as before.

Five weeks passed and I was flat on drugs and homeless again. AJ had been evicted. I made my way to work the square. I walked with my head hanging low, frustrated and miserable. I knew I had been in far more dangerous and life-threatening situations, but the despair in me had become overwhelming. I felt more depressed than ever. It did not matter how much I used, since leaving Victory Outreach I could not even seem to get high anymore, which was really infuriating.

As I passed the nuns' project on Ashley Road, I had this strong inclination that I needed to go back to Victory Outreach. I had this profound sense that I was to be part of something in the future there – I was baffled but felt it deep inside. I crossed the road to go over to the nuns, thinking I would see if they could help me get back to the rehab. Suddenly I experienced an overwhelming sense of hopelessness. It was a sobering moment where I realised that after all these years, I could not fix myself. All my life I had believed I could fix up, but I had failed over thirty-three times to get clean. This was the first time I believed that there really was no hope for me and that this was the end of the road: there was no way out. This was my 'lot in life'. I had chosen this path, and as my mum once said to me, "You've made your bed, now you can lie in it."

I crossed the road and rang the bell of the project. Rosie opened the door, I nearly missed her as she is so tiny.

"Oh, come in dear," she said, and I sheepishly walked in. "Annalise, Trudy is here."

I knew that Annalise was disappointed I had gone past the timeframe that Victory Outreach had given me to be able to go back. Her look said it all. Still, she offered to call the founder on my behalf. Following the call, I sensed she thought I had blown it, as she related that the staff would need to get back to them on a decision.

I headed for work in St Paul's, which was becoming increasingly challenging. The Vice, a police division that focus on narcotics and sex work, were ramping up their presence in the area, which discouraged and slowed down the flow of punters. That night I made an effort and put on a little black skirt and my highest stilettos, desperate to make some money. Times like this, all I needed to pull out all the stops.

It was around half past one in the morning when I headed to Portland Square. As I walked the usual beat, I had this eerie feeling that unnerved me, an inner warning of trouble. I had this random thought: I was going to die, and it was going to be cheap and nasty. I started to walk with a sense of caution as I tentatively looked down the side road. I decided I needed to avoid the dark street. I carried on walking round the square by the streetlights.

"Hey!" I jumped and looked behind me. It was a punter on foot. I was already feeling a little nervous and he put me on edge. He asked for all he could have and said he wanted to go to Castle Park, which was a good ten-minute walk away. I wanted quick transactions, but it was dead and what's more the square was red hot with Vice anyway, so with apprehension and out of desperation I decided to go.

I don't know if he was a set-up, or if the police just followed us, but we were picked up right in front of the camera – funny that! So, I was picked up for indecent exposure, already wanted for breaches of orders and failing to surrender my usual pattern. The result was I was locked up for the night.

The next morning, the key turned in the cell door. "Right, come on, it's time to go."

I was led out to the sweat box to be escorted to court. I was missing my big crucifix. I always had the idea that it was my lucky token – after all, it had seemed to work so many times before, especially as I always prayed in the cells or before court. My name was called, and it was my turn. The cuffs were put on and I was led up the stairs to the magistrate's court and into the dock. I knew I was in trouble and probably would not get out. I had breached my bail too many times and I was 'no fixed abode' now. The three magistrates sat looking at me. The prosecutor had made a good case against me.

"You will be remanded in custody for three weeks and then reappear here whilst pre-sentence reports are being prepared," the lead magistrate said. "Take her down!"

The officer took me by the arms and led me down the stairs back to the cells. I was cold, unwell and desperate for a cigarette. There was nothing worse than not having a smoke, especially heading up to the jail.

Back in the sweat box, I was starting to feel really sick. The journey seemed to take forever; everything takes so much longer when you are withdrawing. I was put on the detox wing, picking up some methadone that could not come quick enough.

I shared a cell with a girl called Chantelle. She had been in nearly a week and was pretty laid back now she was on her meds. She was cool, and shared what tobacco she had with me until it all ran dry and we attempted to roll a cigarette with tea leaves, which was the first and last time I tried that.

I noticed on the wall above my bed there was a calendar hanging in our cell that had Bible verses for every day of the month, and I remember being drawn to read it. I started to come alive when I spoke to Chantelle about the things I was reading and I as read her the day's words, a passion and joy started rising inside me as I attempted to elaborate. Afterwards I lay on top of the itchy blanket on my bed and thought about how good and excited I felt speaking about it. I had no idea that the words in the Bible are more than just ordinary words and have a hidden power behind them. I felt so good as I read them and knew in that moment they were doing me good. Then I recalled I had prayed a prayer to ask Jesus into my heart. It was God's Holy Spirit now living in me that was causing my spirit to get excited about sharing the words I was reading. It was bizarre to me at the time!

While on the detox wing, the chaplain came to my cell and told me I had a call. It was Dinah, the founder of Victory Outreach. The nuns had got wind of me being back in the jail and they had spoken to Dinah about the chance of me going back. On the phone, she asked me if I wanted to come home. *Home!* She was warm yet firm, and told me that if I wanted to, she would be willing to write a letter to support an application for bail to the rehab. She offered to send someone to court to support me in the process. I went silent as she spoke; deep down I felt a resistance and really didn't want to go back. Yet here she was on the phone, freely and willingly offering to support me. I needed time to think about it.

"I will think about it and let you know. Can you give me some time to get back to you?"

She agreed. I wasn't ready to say yes. It was a get out of jail card, but I was not sure I wanted the trade-off. The thought of that restriction on my life made me feel trapped. As the chaplain took me back to my cell, I walked almost in silence. The chaplain tried to encourage me that this was a good opportunity and to take my time to think about it, reminding me I would need to let them know soon.

Arriving back at my cell, it felt like a weight on me, that sobering feeling again. I knew on the inside that I was on the cusp of something. I felt as though I had a life changing decision to make. I wrestled for three days about what I would do. One part of me just wanted to get out and go and use, to get high one more time! Anything that restricted me from being free to do what I wanted seemed oppressive and confining to me. Little did I realise then that this interpretation of freedom had led me to be a prisoner: a prisoner to rebellion, addiction, prostitution, crime, greed and selfishness. Every time I would drift off and think about making the decision to refuse Dinah's offer to go back to Victory Outreach, I felt myself hit an invisible brick wall, as though something was stopping me from going any further. At the time I didn't understand it, but there is no doubt for me now that this was the Spirit of God wanting to lead me into freedom.

I moved from the detox wing over to the E wing. My pad mate got out, so I had the cell and my little TV to myself, which had its advantages. With Akon blasting, these lyrics struck me, playing over and over in my mind that last week I was in there:

> These streets remind me of quicksand
> When you're on it, you will keep goin' down,
> And there is no one to hold on to
> And there is no one to pull you out
> You keep on fallin' and no one can hear you callin'
> So, you end up self-destructin' …
> Teeth marks on my back from the K-9 …
> You gotta be willin' to pray
> Yes, there gotta be, there gotta be another way…

I knew there had to be another way, and that being clean was helping me to begin to think differently. I liked having my own cell. I had some money and tobacco, that was good enough for now – I could try and get some gear later. I filled an application to the chapel as it meant getting out of my cell. The chaplain started to speak about how much Jesus cared for us. One of the girls in front of me was mocking throughout the service, which made me so angry inside. When we got out of the service and we were waiting to get back to the wing, I couldn't contain it anymore.

"That was really disrespectful, mocking like that!" I blurted out. She was taken aback. Maybe it was the boldness and strength seeming to flow out of me that made her a bit stunned. I was left thinking, *That's not like me*. The officer came out of the chapel, keys rattling.

"Let's go, come on, all those for E wing."

Nobody said another word about it, there was just the usual banter on the way back to the wing. I was still shocked. *What was all that about?*

I had another visit from the chaplain about Victory Outreach. I didn't mess about: my answer was yes. I was trying to get my head around the decision, but I felt better now I had made it. When my day for court arrived, I was still on my methadone and Valium. I was woken by officers unlocking my door early; it was barely light through my cell window.

"Meds, come on, let's go," the officer instructed me.

As I left my cell to go at six that morning, there were the usual shouts.

"Good luck, Trudy, make sure you don't come back!"

"Have a smoke for me!"

I was now ready for the sweat box. I picked up my plastic prison bag from reception with everything I owned in there. I was feeling nervous: my belly was doing somersaults, I had no idea how it would go. I did not want to get my hopes up and wondered if I had made the right call. I was starting to want to get out and to get clean now.

The officer brought me up the old wooden staircase from the cells to the court with cuffs on. Escorting me into the dock, the officer unlocked the cuffs. To my right were the three magistrates, staring back at me. As I looked over the room, I spotted Sue, the house manager at Victory Outreach, Sue was about four foot four, with short dark hair and a serious-looking face. I wondered if she ever smiled. Last time she took me to Bristol, I did a runner. Looking at her, I felt a heavy feeling coming over me. Her serious intention for me to make correct choices from now on was written all over her face. I felt all I wanted in that moment was a hug or a nod of acceptance, and I failed to see that her being present was all that I needed.

"Can the defendant please stand? You are charged with possession of a class A drug, namely heroin, obtaining property by deception, theft and the handling of stolen goods, failing to surrender on seven accounts to custody at an appointed time, and breaching of a Drug Testing Order. Can the defendant state full name, date of birth, and address?"

"Trudy Amanda Makepeace, 14th February 1973, NFA."

"Do you plead guilty or not guilty?"

"Guilty."

"The defendant can be seated," said the magistrate in the middle.

I sat down on the hard wooden seat, facing the clear shield before me. As I sat there, everything became a bit of a blur: all I could think about was what life would be like if I went back to Victory Outreach and I started to feel deflated once again as I considered the rules and restrictions that would be imposed on return.

Following some pre-sentence reports and the letter from Dinah that was presented to support my application, the court decided to give me a six-month conditional residency order. I was to return in six months for sentencing.

Sue was waiting for me as I came out of the holding cell. I signed at the desk to get my things and the oversized clear prison bag as they released me into her care. As we left, she gave me a sideways glance and a smile.

"I wasn't sure if you were going to run off," she said to me in the car. "I could see you were struggling in the court."

"Was I that easy to read?"

Evidently, I was. She had read me right. Yet here I was. I had chosen the right way forward, although I can't say it felt like it at the time. I had to go against my instincts.

Chapter 23: Fresh Start

I didn't talk much on the drive back to Wales. I was mulling over having a clean break from AJ and everything that had just happened in court. I knew this was it this time, I would need to stick it out. We arrived back at Victory Outreach. This time I had only my prison bag that carried the few items I had to my name, the tiny black skirt I was arrested in and my studded six-inch stilettos. Thankfully I'd picked up some jeans and a t-shirt in the jail. Everyone was warm and welcoming, and it was nice to see some of their faces again. I was put in a room to share with Carole again, and I was pleased about that, as she made me laugh.

"Trudy, you look like someone from a concentration camp." she said in a gentle manner. *A bit extreme*, I thought, but it was true that I was as grey as the pavement and only skin and bone. It took months for me to begin to look remotely human again.

I soon settled in and adapted quickly back into the program – it helped pass the time as I knew I was here to stay for the next six months at least. Towards the end of my detox, I was moved into my own room. It was a sign that I was generally progressing well, but I still had the mindset of an addict. I was anxious about coming off the final small dose of Valium, although it was such a minor amount that any withdrawals were more related to my psychological dependency now.

It was during this time up in my cosy attic room that I picked up the 'Father's Love Letter', which Laine, another resident in the rehab, had handed me earlier in the day. I had been curious to read it earlier, but had been busy on a work program. Later whilst alone that night I picked it up and settled down to read it.

My Child,

You may not know me, but I know everything about you. (Psalm 139:1)
I know when you sit down and when you rise up. (Psalm 139:2)
I am familiar with all your ways. (Psalm 139:3)
Even the very hairs on your head are numbered. (Matthew 10:29-31)
For you were made in my image. (Genesis 1:27)
In me you live and move and have your being. (Acts 17:28)
For you are my offspring. (Acts 17:28)
I knew you even before you were conceived. (Jeremiah 1:4-5)
I chose you when I planned creation. (Ephesians 1:11-12)
You were not a mistake, for all your days are written in my book. (Psalm 139:15-16)
I determined the exact time of your birth and where you would live. (Acts 17:26)
You are fearfully and wonderfully made. (Psalm 139:14)
I knit you together in your mother's womb. (Psalm 139:13)
And brought you forth on the day you were born. (Psalm 71:6)
I have been misrepresented by those who don't know me. (John 8:41-44)
I am not distant and angry, but am the complete expression of love. (1 John 4:16)
And it is my desire to lavish my love on you. (1 John 3:1)
Simply because you are my child and I am your Father. (1 John 3:1)

I offer you more than your earthly father ever could. (Matthew 7:11)
For I am the perfect father. (Matthew 5:48)
Every good gift that you receive comes from my hand. (James 1:17)
For I am your provider and I meet all your needs. (Matthew 6:31-33)
My plan for your future has always been filled with hope. (Jeremiah 29:11)
Because I love you with an everlasting love. (Jeremiah 31:3)
My thoughts toward you are countless as the sand on the seashore. (Psalm 139:17-18)
And I rejoice over you with singing. (Zephaniah 3:17)
I will never stop doing good to you. (Jeremiah 32:40)
For you are my treasured possession. (Exodus 19:5)
I desire to establish you with all my heart and all my soul. (Jeremiah 32:41)
And I want to show you great and marvellous things. (Jeremiah 33:3)
If you seek me with all your heart, you will find me. (Deuteronomy 4:29)
Delight in me and I will give you the desires of your heart. (Psalm 37:4)
For it is I who gave you those desires. (Philippians 2:13)
I am able to do more for you than you could possibly imagine. (Ephesians 3:20)
For I am your greatest encourager. (2 Thessalonians 2:16-17)
I am also the Father who comforts you in all your troubles. (2 Corinthians 1:3-4)
When you are brokenhearted, I am close to you. (Psalm 13:18)
As a shepherd carries a lamb, I have carried you close to my heart. (Isaiah 40:11)

One day I will wipe away every tear from your eyes. (Revelation 21:3-4)
And I'll take away all the pain you have suffered on this earth. (Revelation 21:3-4)
I am your Father, and I love you even as I love my son, Jesus. (John 17:23)
For in Jesus, my love for you is revealed. (John 17:26)
He is the exact representation of my being. (Hebrews 1:3)
He came to demonstrate that I am for you, not against you. (Romans 8:31)
And to tell you that I am not counting your sins. (2 Corinthians 5:18-19)
Jesus died so that you and I could be reconciled. (2 Corinthians 5:18-19)
His death was the ultimate expression of my love for you. (1 John 4:10)
I gave up everything I loved that I might gain your love. (Romans 8:31-32)
If you receive the gift of my son Jesus, you receive me. (1 John 2:23)
And nothing will ever separate you from my love again. (Romans 8:38-39)
Come home and I'll throw the biggest party heaven has ever seen. (Luke 15:7)
I have always been Father, and will always be Father. (Ephesians 3:14-15)
My question is…Will you be my child? (John 1:12-13)
I am waiting for you. (Luke 15:11-32)

Love, Your Dad.
Almighty God

Engrossed in the letter, I felt a warm sensation filling my heart. I sensed God was speaking directly to me like He was right there in the room with me. I connected deeply with the words on the page and my heart softened; I began to feel this incredible compassion and disarming love with its irresistible warm embrace, causing my heart to expand and open up to His voice through every word on the page.

I had never felt more alive, or known anything that felt so pure and true. In that moment, my heart and my spirit knew this was real. It was the most beautiful and real thing I had experienced in a long time. I had this inner sense of knowing that I had truly come home, that I had been lost and was now found. Despite everything I had done, He offered me this unconditional love even though I knew I did not deserve such love and kindness.

Finishing the letter and putting it down, I realised that everything I had been searching and looking for was found in God: love, acceptance, security, belonging, forgiveness, and hope, through his son Jesus. Up until that point, I had not even realised I was looking, seeking life and satisfaction in drugs, relationships, money, status and the acceptance and love of others.

I was overwhelmed by the love I felt from God. My mind wandered back to the fact I never knew my real father and the deep longing I had to know him. As I sat reading these words, I felt like God knew this and revealed Himself in this way as the ultimate Father, especially for me. This discovery of this love and acceptance for me superseded any expectations I had of an earthly father. I felt a release, and suddenly the questions about my biological father just did not matter to me anymore.

I sat on the end of the bed as I finished reading the letter. For a moment, the thought popped into my head: *Is this real, or am I being brainwashed?* I knew deep down, though, that I had made a mess of trying to do life my way. I was desperate. I had reached the end of my own strength, ability and resources; I felt powerless to change myself and completely worn out trying.

I got down on my knees at the end of my bed and could feel the room was full of love. I prayed, wholeheartedly asking Jesus into my life, asking for His forgiveness. This time, it was personal. I more fully understood what he had done on the cross and why. I decided I would trust Him to help me with my whole life.

After my prayer and decision to trust Him, I realised the crushing weight that I had been carrying had completely gone. It was unexplainable, unfathomable to my natural mind. I experienced a peace coming into my heart and filling the room like I had never known. Before that moment, all I had ever known was restlessness, anxiety, and a fear about being still. Waves of love seemed to wash over me, I knew complete acceptance and I felt I had found home, a place where I belonged. I felt safe and secure.

I felt clean on the inside, as though I had just an inner bath. I felt pure, like a virgin again. *How is this even possible?* I sat and pondered, trying to work out where that load had gone. I realised I had experienced forgiveness. No one could forgive me like that but God. The blood of Jesus, which was shed on the cross for us, cleanses us from all unrighteousness and purifies us from all sin. All those men, the streets, the parlours… I was clean. A priceless gift.

I experienced His mercy: my guilt and the shame were removed, my dignity restored instantly. It almost seemed unfair, that I should walk free, yet it was a reality – my reality, as I received Jesus Christ as my Saviour. I lay down in peace, contemplating my new discovery.

Over the coming weeks I realised that what seemed like a bigger miracle was apparent. I stopped the Valium and realised I was free from the controlling power and grip of addiction. This was evidence to me that God was real. I had been a slave to drugs for years; I had been possessed by my need and drive for drugs. The desire to pick up a needle, a crack pipe or any other drug was gone. This was the miracle that spoke to me the loudest, and overnight I was released.

I felt a love like I had never known. I felt safe, secure, accepted, loved. I had found the greatest love of all: that of my Father in heaven. This love brought me hope, hope for a future. I would soon discover that this hope would release me from the pain and struggles of my past and they would no longer dictate my future. I knew that my life would never be the same again. This was even more than a fresh start: it was a new beginning. This was my miracle!

It was becoming more apparent as the days went on that Jesus Christ had released me from many of my old behaviours that controlled my life: not only was I free from addiction, but also from lying, lust, sexual immorality, greed, selfishness, stealing, anger, bitterness and manipulation.

I had a conviction to get rid of the few items I had that were stolen and related to my old life. I knew God was asking me to get rid of them, that they were no longer a part of the new life I was experiencing. I had been a compulsive liar to aid me in my escapades, but now there was no room for lies. It was as though God's spirit in me compelled me to tell the truth, even when I felt embarrassed. The ongoing lust and desire to be sexually gratified that had a grip on me was broken. I had a new perspective and desire for pure intimacy. I stopped swearing. There was no doubt that things had changed – I had changed. What I had tried unsuccessfully to accomplish for years miraculously began overnight with a simple but honest prayer.

It was a while later that one of the directors of the rehab was reminiscing and said, "When you first came in, I took one look at you and thought, 'she'll never make it.'"

He had taken one look at my extreme brokenness and sadly he felt there was no hope for me! Even the most destitute, broken, and vilest offender can find hope in the arms of a saviour.

Now my heart was clean, my mouth was clean, and I felt different. I had also gained some new desires. I wanted to know Jesus more, I had a hunger to read His words, to speak to Him, to get close to Him. I wanted to lock myself away to be with Him. I loved His presence with me. I recall reading in the Bible how God had adopted me into His family. It was easy for me to embrace this, as I so easily identified with it. I found a huge sense of acceptance, belonging and security in discovering this truth, as I had the sense he was far more reliable and dependable than anyone else I had known.

Chapter 24: Transformed

"I can't believe how much weight I have put on," I muttered to myself. Within a few months, I had gone from six to eight stone. I lay on my bed, feeling uncomfortable and heavy with the weight.

"Come on the noo," Carole said in her Scottish accent. "Dinnae forget what you were like, you look so much better now aye, Trudy. Ya looked like someone fae a concentration camp when you came in, aye. Och, ya needed to put on weight. Ach, you were so thin and looked as grey as the pavement, like the walking deid."

Surely, I wasn't that bad? It was a sobering thought, but I still had a long way to go, I knew. Even though I had put weight on, my skin and colour was still not healthy. As I sat cross-legged on the bed looking over at Carole, who had also obviously gained weight, I knew I had to make my peace with this new reality. Sighing, I lay back on the bed with my head on the cushioned pillow, looking up at the ceiling. I knew the truth was that what had been my normal was abnormal.

I recalled to mind how much God loved me and that His commitment to my wellbeing and wholeness meant my body, too. I considered His words, that I was fearfully and wonderfully made just the way I was. I had discovered a new-found freedom and confidence to be the real me that He had always intended me to be. It was a liberating decision. It was the truth and hope of both these things that helped me to accept the new changes happening in my body.

This new-found acceptance I had discovered in God's love helped me to gain my value and confidence in how God made me and what

He said, rather than my distorted perspective or the world's view and constantly trying to fit into my idea of the perfect size.

As the months passed, I realised that God was restoring me. I recognised and became more familiar and accepting of the girl who had been buried under years of being lost to addiction and everything that came with it. My relationship with Jesus completely changed my heart: towards Him, towards others, and in my perspective for the future. Every challenge of the journey was worthwhile in the light of this new discovery and hope He had promised, as I had read a prophecy in the Bible:

> *"For I know the plans I have for you ... plans to give you a hope and a future."* (Jeremiah 29:11)

I knew this new life was the only thing I had worth living for. Five months into my time at Victory Outreach, I had come face to face with the reality of the brokenness that was in my life and just how detrimental many of my choices had been. I knew others had wronged me, but I too had been responsible for a lot of pain. As the times I had stolen, lied and cheated others came to mind, I felt convicted and saw my part in these things; irrespective of what had happened to me, I had caused a lot of damage. I was truly sorry for the wrongs I had done.

The more I read God's word, the more I saw His goodness and kindness and my need of His forgiveness. One evening, I was reading some passages in the Bible and realised just how much my behaviour had hurt Him and others and how much I needed the Lord's forgiveness, healing and strengthening. I suddenly saw His goodness in contrast to my sin.

It was as I read Psalm 51 that my heart broke. I realised I had grieved God as I read these words:

> *"Have mercy upon me, O God, because of your unfailing love. Because of your great compassion, blot out the stain of my sins. Wash me clean from my guilt. Purify me from my sin. For I recognise my rebellion; it haunts me day and night. Against you and you alone have I sinned; I have done what is evil in your sight. You will be proved right in what you say, and your judgement against me is just."* (Psalm 51:1-4 NLT)

The tears of regret and pain rolled down my face; I was discovering a deeper, profound sense of my own sinfulness and God's forgiveness. It was then as I spoke and poured out my heart to Him I realised that there was so much brokenness than ran deeper that I was able to articulate. My whole life, my emotions, my thoughts, my heart and my soul had been impacted through years of pain, destructive behaviour, and harmful sinful patterns that had formed in my life. As I continued to read, these verses began to jump out at me:

> *"Purify me from my sins, and I will be clean; wash me, and I will be whiter than snow... Remove the stain of my guilt. Create in me a clean heart, O God. Renew a loyal spirit within me ... don't take your Holy Spirit from me."* (Psalm 51:7-11 NLT)

As I finished reading, I asked Him to create in me a clean heart, as the psalmist did, and I took comfort in the words, *'the sacrifice you desire is a broken spirit'.* I knew my spirit had been broken, but now it was broken by the recognition of my sin and His word assured me that He would not reject a broken and repentant heart, one that was sincere enough to change. That day, I made a decision in line with a verse that jumped out at me from the Bible:

> *"If you are a thief, quit stealing. Instead, use your hands for good hard work, and then give generously to others in need."* (Ephesians 4:28 NLT)

This realisation that it had taken me thirty-three years to get to this point helped me to understand that unravelling my pain, and the damage it had done, would take time. I had peace, and this truth helped me to accept and be patient with myself and to allow Jesus to hold me as I healed. Just like any wound that needs to be cleaned and bandaged to protect it as it heals, Jesus is the one who heals the broken in heart and binds up our wounds in the process. I was learning to continually trust Him with the unknown, with my anxieties about the next steps. I learned to lean on Him sharing my concerns and requests for help one day at a time.

At Victory Outreach, the residents were given house chores, including cooking and cleaning. This was meant to help us learn basic life skills and instil a work ethic. I attended three meetings a day, where we would pray and read the Bible together, talking at length about the verses and reflecting on the relevance and how we could apply God's Word practically to our lives. This was not just to inform, but to transform our hearts, also to enable our minds to be renewed. It was a chance to build on the discovery of these profound truths instead of building only on my own ideas, experiences, hurts, or even what others said.

It was a Friday morning. Friday was the day when Laura used to come in and speak to us during the morning meeting. She was a petite woman, very unassuming and gentle. She must have been in her mid to late sixties. She used to go into the schools and teach the children about Jesus. I loved it when she came. It was as though she had a direct hotline to God! Without fail, she would speak directly into what was happening in the house or what was going on in our lives. I learned that it was her prayer life that meant she was able to hear God's voice and be led by Him. I was fascinated with her stories of answered prayer and admired her evidently close relationship with Jesus. I longed to hear and experience God in the way that she did.

Laura began to speak about a story that Jesus told. It was about a woman who was sick and in a hopeless situation until she met Jesus. She said how the woman had tried everything to fix herself, that she used all her resources: money, doctors, and her own ideas, until she literally had nothing left and had run out of hope, strength, money and options. She sounded just like me. I knew what it meant to have come to the end of myself. The woman, like me, found hope in a hopeless place and that hope was Jesus: He had helped her and healed her.

Then as she read the story, she repeated the words of Jesus:

> *"Daughter, your faith has made you well. Go in peace. Your suffering is over."* (Mark 5:34 NLT)

My heart was quickened, and I knew that Jesus was speaking directly to me. I would come to learn that faith and salvation in Jesus means you are healed and set free. Jesus healed her, set her free from shame, and restored her dignity.

I was due to return to court, as my six months probationary period had almost passed. It was these words that morning that brought me strength, faith, assurance and peace about who I now was as His daughter. I was at peace and confident that everything was going to be ok. When Jesus speaks to us personally, it changes everything – it changes us.

Sue, the house manager, was anxious: I had run off the last time I had gone to Bristol while at Victory Outreach. I knew she was wondering if I might run off again. I was taken over to see the managing director for a final pep talk to put everyone's mind at ease. I was overflowing with confidence that everything was going to be just fine, but it seemed I was the only one who was.

We travelled the following week. As we boarded the train early that morning, the air was cold and sharp as it caught my face, helping me to wake up more fully. I started to get butterflies again when the engine chugged and the train moved away from the platform. I always got them when I was nervous, apprehensive or when I wanted to use drugs. It was like the old adrenaline started to pump around my body. I reminded myself things were different this time. I found a new strength in the desire for the new thing God was doing in my life, and gradually the negative feelings and nerves died down.

We arrived at the court and, as we walked up the stairs to the court, I recognised a few faces. I passed by Clyde, who was tall and thin from smoking so much crack. I knew him from the road, not massively well, but we had scored and smoked crack together.

"Good to see you, Trudy! You're looking well," he said.

"Hey, Clyde!"

It was typical that I would see someone. I could sense Sue's anxiety as we spoke.

"Hey, fancy coming for a smoke?"

"Not today, Clyde," I replied with boldness and confidence. "I don't do that anymore. I'm sorting myself out."

It felt good. I felt ten feet tall, I could hardly believe that those words had come out of my mouth. I walked by without a temptation to go, and it felt good.

Before I knew it, it was my turn. The court usher called my name. I stepped into the courtroom and into the dock and stood before the bench.

"Please take a seat!"

As I sat down, I realised I was sitting in front of the same bench I was in front of six months ago. The same three faces were staring right back at me. My solicitor came over to confirm that they were going to be asking for a residency order for Victory Outreach.

"Can the defendant please stand?" As I stood, he addressed me. "State for the court your full name and date of birth and address."

"Trudy Amanda Makepeace, 14th February 1973, Victory Outreach, Tredegar."

"On your last appearance, you pleaded guilty to the following charges: possession of a class A drug, namely heroin, obtaining property by deception, theft and the handling of stolen goods, failing to surrender to custody at the appointed time, three accounts breaching your DTTO, and indecent exposure. Today you are here for us to pass sentence, do you understand?"

"Yes."

"Please sit down."

As they read through the documents presented to them, one of the magistrates asked me what I was doing at the home. I had been enrolled in some basic English classes and a computer course whilst at the rehab. Dinah had given me a glowing report on my progress, also proposing plans for me to embark on a full-time college course.

"You are not the same person that stood before us six months ago," the magistrate said. He commented on how I looked and sounded different. I was stunned they even remembered me. His words were more significant than he knew. This was a new day, another new chapter in my life. My spirit skipped a beat when he said those words. My heart was full of gratitude for the change in my heart and life so far.

The magistrates left the courtroom to confer on passing sentence. I took a deep breath. My solicitor invited Sue to come over to the dock.

"I think it looks positive," he said. I was still apprehensive, but I had that faith and peace that Jesus was with me and was on my side.

"Will the court please rise?"

They were back already. Instead of the usual racing of my heart, I stood up before them with peace inside.

"We acknowledge that you are not the same girl that stood before us six months ago, and in light of your good progress, of which we do not want to hinder, we have decided you should continue at Victory Outreach. Therefore, for the crimes you have committed, the court will defer sentence with a conditional discharge for one year, with a condition of residency to reside at Victory Outreach for eighteen months. We want to take the opportunity to say well done and wish you well for your future."

I could barely take it in. I tried to process that I was going to have to stay at Victory Outreach for eighteen months, which felt like a life sentence. At the same time, I was so excited because they recognised the transformation that had taken place in me.

The Word of God says that anyone who is in Christ is a new creation; the old has passed and everything has become new. That was me. I felt brand new. My old life was firmly behind me and I had been given a fresh start to live in the power of Christ so that I could live differently.

Not only that, but I had also refused a smoke of crack and was successfully back on the train to Wales with joy and peace in my heart. We got to the train station and as we walked to the car, I could see the relief on Sue's face.

"I wasn't sure you wouldn't run off again!" she said.

I knew she was remembering the last time when I had legged it back to Bristol. I had the confidence that the Lord had spoken to me and that I would return, but evidently it takes time for us to regain others' confidence.

Chapter 25: New Life

Arriving back at the rehab, I burst through the door – I couldn't wait to share what had happened! I was more excited than anyone by the fact that the judge had acknowledged my transformation.

"That's great news that they could see the difference in you!" Michelle, a staff member, commented encouragingly. She had seen the mess I was in when I arrived on previous occasions.

Considering the day's events, the prospect of a further eighteen months on top of the six months I had already been there seemed a bit steep.

"That's a bit much! I can't believe they give you that long, I can't imagine having to be here for that amount of time," commented another one of the girls, as she heard my result. But I knew I had got off lightly even if it didn't feel like it. I knew if I left Victory Outreach, they would throw the book at me. The one thing that helped me get my head around it was that I wanted to continue the journey and explore this new life in Christ.

During that time, I continued to feel the intense reality of God's love in my heart and His close companionship with me. I discovered that God's love is pure, and unconditional – that He wanted me, He chose me, and He had adopted me:

> *"God decided in advance to adopt us into his own family by bringing us to himself through Jesus Christ. This is what he wanted to do and it gave him great pleasure."* (Romans 1:5 NLT)

Having been adopted as a child, I was familiar with how it works, but this time there was a difference: in my new position in His family I felt an incredible sense of security. I knew that I belonged, that I was accepted, and that the very things that I had longed for growing up were found and made complete in Him.

From this place I began the journey of walking out my healing. Broken but full of hope, a bad day in rehab was still better than a good day on the streets. I had already experienced such a level of freedom from things that held me a prisoner and I knew this was just the beginning. *One day at a time,* I would remind myself as the time passed. Sometimes it dragged and then it would go fast, but what was evident was that it would not be a quick journey. As my good friend says, 'God is not a microwave God.'

There were times I really struggled with being in rehab: the rules, the staff, the other girls rubbing each other up the wrong way, but it was a place where all the wrong distractions were cut off. I needed those boundaries with tight restrictions to enable me to get stronger and to be able to deal with temptations, discipline and personal responsibility. Gradually I was learning how to consider others above myself, which was all made so much more joyful by God's presence at work in my heart.

On Sundays we attended a small local church. One morning, as we were leaving after the service, I picked up a Christian newspaper, then hesitantly I went to put it back as there were only two left. The pastor, who was on the door saying his goodbyes, picked it up and put in my hand.

"Take it," he insisted. "It's for you, I want you to have it."

"Okay, thanks," I said as I took it from his hands.

I arrived home and, as I was waiting for our Sunday dinner, I started reading this paper. Right there, spread over two pages, was Remi! I could not believe my eyes. It really was her; I would recognise her and that gold tooth anywhere. I had prayed for Remi when I arrived at Victory Outreach, thinking she would be the last person in the world to get saved, the hardest to reach. I knew the Lord had reached me, yet I still doubted she would turn to Him, that He could reach her. Now here I was in the back of nowhere, astounded that this Christian paper I was holding had covered her story – and centre-spread worthy it was, too! She was fostering and teaching; her life had been radically transformed after meeting with Jesus in Holloway prison. She had left Holloway and gone to Victory International in London. I was so encouraged.

Since that day, I have never doubted God's ability to reach anyone, especially those that seem the hardest to reach. I watched her give her testimony on YouTube a few years later. She looked like Remi, but she sounded like someone I had never known; the transformation was mind-blowing to me at the time. I saw how God had brought us both to a place where all the rubbish we had picked up in life, the behaviours and attitudes that came with life's choices and experiences, had been removed and we were brought back to a place of God's design for our lives. I could see that both of us were in a place where others could see the real person and all that God had put within us. Personalities and giftings were coming to light, all making us unique. I was so encouraged how God had orchestrated this in a small valley in the middle of South Wales.

Being back at the rehab meant that I had to see the GP about the Hepatitis C, which had been flagged up the last time. I lay in bed reflecting and thinking that I had no right to ask God to heal me. I had Hep C due to my own irresponsible actions – in fact, I considered myself fortunate that that was all I had. As I pondered these things, I felt Jesus whisper into my heart that I should ask Him to heal me. I knew it was Him, because it was not in my thoughts to ask. His voice was always so recognisable: kind, tender and affirming. He whispered again. This time,

I knew I should ask Him to heal me despite the fact that I had already judged myself unworthy. He wanted me to ask! Within His invitation to ask was a profound sense of love and warmth, almost as though He was teaching me about who He is, as a good father.

I said sorry for my actions, even though that wasn't a condition of His desire to heal me. I felt so grateful for His love; I never wanted to hurt Him. I felt deeply sorry for my previous behaviour and actions, not least because I'd ignored Him in the life I had lived. Now, despite all of that, because He was my Father, He was offering to heal me. So, I asked. After my visit to the GP they took more bloods, and they came back negative! I had no doubt, Jesus had healed me. Over the years I've wanted to be sure I really was healed and was tested several times, each time discovering that I really do not have Hepatitis C.

Jesus taught me about His compassion and kindness towards me as I continued through rehab, providing for me many times. Sometimes it was simple things. For example, I really wanted a decent pair of trainers and some clothes, as I had nothing much. I asked Him, and the next day I was given some brand new trainers and two bags of clothes. Even the quiet longings and desires of my heart, He gave before I asked. During my time there, I recall thinking I would love to learn to ride a horse. Within a few weeks, I was offered the opportunity to go horse riding. I learned it is His delight to show us His goodness and love towards us.

I knew my life was forever marked. I would never be the same again, God's power and presence at work in my life was more precious and real to me than anything else had ever been in my life. I grew hungry to know God more. I was still chaotic and muddled in my mind, but He never was.

One evening, I read a passage in the Bible about being baptised. I realised that it was an act of faith in obedience to Christ. Baptism identifies us with Jesus' death and resurrection: as we go into the water, it's symbolic of dying to the old life and coming up again raised to a new life in Christ. I was desperate to obey Jesus' words, to believe and be baptised. When I realised I would have to wait months, I decided to baptise myself in the bath!

At the start of my journey in Victory Outreach, I struggled to communicate. Firstly, I could not talk about the past. I simply didn't know how to, due to the pain and a lack of ability to process and reflect constructively. Secondly, I still was overshadowed by feelings of insignificance, worthlessness, shame and the belief that nobody would want to listen to me anyway. As a result, I struggled to connect and communicate what I felt on a deeper level and what I thought regarding my own situation and circumstances.

The only thing I could communicate with confidence was anything Jesus spoke or revealed to me through His Word as it applies in the here and now. He became my counsellor, my closest confidant and best friend.

Now the time had arrived when it was announced Victory Outreach would be having a baptism. *Better late than never,* I thought. Sue approached me one day.

"Trudy, Dinah has asked for you to share your story of coming to faith."

My heart dropped. Suddenly I was full of butterflies, nerves and fears. I could not believe she had asked me. My mind wandered back to when I had first arrived and was asked to say a brief hello and something about coming to Victory Outreach in a church meeting. I could not speak; my brokenness was far too raw to speak about without breaking. Now, nine months later, I was finally able to be baptised and this would be the first time to share my story so far. I wanted to do it.

Being baptised was a real act of commitment for me. It was me showing the world that I was dedicating my life to Jesus, who loved me, rescued me and set me free. I was privileged to be asked, but the prospect was daunting. All week I prayed constantly for His help, presence, and strength to speak.

The day finally arrived. It felt sacred, like a wedding day: as I prepared my heart and spent time with Him, I knew I was wholeheartedly committing to a lifelong relationship. As we arrived at the church, to my astonishment the three nuns were there. Dinah had arranged for them to come as a surprise, as she knew they had been pretty much my only support. My sister Marie came, as she had just recently visited me at the rehab after she found me through missing persons.

I got up, and I spoke with a new-found courage. It was as if I had the boldness of a lion, I knew it was the Lord Jesus empowering me. I think we were all astounded. As I recounted some of my journey and explained that it was literally by the grace of God that I was even alive, I saw my sister completely break and tears flood down her face. I had to look away in order to keep going, or I too would have wept. That day I experienced God's power and presence in a profound way. I gained new confidence in speaking out. If there was one thing in all my life I was sure of, it was that Jesus had found me and rescued me according to His great mercy and kindness. I knew Jesus had begun to restore my voice because I had a deep contentment about being heard. Something inside me was beginning to ease; my striving ceased because I knew I was put on this planet with a purpose to be heard and seen. That was a giant leap away from the childhood message I'd received and believed for years.

During my time in the home, I fell more and more in love with Jesus. I was captivated: I knew He was with me in everything I did, whether that was carrying out a chore, or whether it was my response or attitude in a situation. I had so much gratitude in my heart towards Him that I wanted to live in a way that would please Him – not that I had to prove myself, but because I was so in love with Jesus, I was intent on doing the right thing and honouring Him. I had finally discovered the strength of real love and I wanted my behaviour to reflect my love. I hoped never to hurt or offend Jesus or anyone else from that point onward. Ephesians 5:1 (NLT) says, *'Imitate God, therefore, in everything you do, because you are his dear children.'* I was determined to do this.

For so long, I had lived to please myself – wild and rebellious, living for drugs and momentary pleasures – but all my pleasure-seeking always left me emptier and more broken. Now I had discovered such an intimate friendship with God Himself, and I found it truly amazing that God would see fit to make Himself known and befriend me in this way.

I had profound times of worshipping in his presence: I'd play worship music in my bedroom, and I would kneel or pace my room thanking God, singing out my heart to Him, or lying down allowing the music to wash over me. I had prolonged times in prayer where I would talk to Him, share my concerns, or pray for others. I would use the Bible to help me to see what He was like and speak to Him as I read the Bible.

Through those times I felt closer to Him, entwined with Him. I found Him speaking to me more and more through His word, which began to liberate me from the lies I had believed and had accepted about who I was. Other times, I would feel prompted strongly to step out in faith and share the word with others. I learned to partner with Him and listen to Him through reading His word.

As I read the Bible, I realised that my life did not need to be determined by my negative feelings. I could choose what to think about and my plans did not need to be led or dictated by my emotions any longer. I had always believed if I felt rubbish, I was rubbish, and therefore behaved in ways that confirmed that I was rubbish. If I felt worthless, I would dwell on thoughts that fed that emotion, which had resulted in me becoming more bound to the lies of being of no value. Now I was learning to accept His truth that I was valued, allowing Him to shape my view of myself, not circumstances, the past and others' opinions.

Of course, now that I was clean, my emotions were like a rollercoaster. I was reminded of my fluctuating emotions as a teenager, although at least now I was experiencing more ups than downs!

Discovering that I could separate what I thought about from how I felt was a revolutionary concept to me, even at the age of thirty-three. It was as though a massive light bulb went on. I learned that while I may still have negative feelings, I did not need to be controlled by them. I could renew my mind by choosing to believe the truth of the Word of God and applying what God says, rather than letting my emotions lead the way. My heart was changing in its impulses and desires and my mind was grasping a new way of living. The Bible says:

> *"Do not be conformed to the world (any longer with its superficial values and customs), but be transformed and progressively changed (as you mature spiritually) by the renewing of your mind (focusing on godly values and ethical attitudes), so that you may prove (for yourselves) what the will of God is, that which is good, acceptable and perfect (in His plan and purpose for you)."* (Romans 12:2 AMP)

While on the programme at Victory Outreach, I continued attending and completing short courses, which gave me a sense of confidence, progression and learning. I felt the need to grow in other areas of my life. I was keen to develop throughout my recovery. Every small achievement helped me to embrace bigger opportunities and challenges that were to come, requiring commitment, perseverance and discipline.

Chapter 26: Learning to Trust

It was my first New Year's clean. All the staff and the men and women of the rehab had come together to celebrate the New Year, sharing stories and giving thanks to God. It was really moving.

When I spoke, however, I announced with real conviction, "I still don't trust anyone."

The statement just came out and it was true. Out of the heart the mouth speaks. During my first year at Victory Outreach, it was evident that I had major trust issues. I was comfortable trusting God when it was just me and Him. I felt safe with Him, but I was unable to let anyone else get too close to me, much less really trust them or emotionally connect with them. I was by nature now a rescuer, an encourager, someone who believed in and fought for others. Yet I always kept people at arm's length. I had become so guarded; I believed that if people really knew me then they might reject me, or that if I made myself vulnerable then they could become a threat to my new life. It was much easier to maintain relationship on my terms.

That said, I loved to encourage and befriend people that came into the programme, to support and help them. In fact, I especially loved to help those who seemed the hardest to reach, those that others viewed as difficult. I wanted to fight for them and for them to believe and come through as I had.

"You're different," Carla had once said as we cleaned the minibus. She had not long been in the home and was still sussing everyone out. "I've been watching you."

I learned that people could see something of Jesus in me. It meant I could encourage and share with them how Jesus had changed me and answer some of their questions. I found such a passion and joy in speaking about Him, it made me come alive more fully.

Nearly a year had passed. Over time, I started to feel convicted about telling people that Jesus had set me free when I was still addicted to smoking cigarettes. I wanted to prove the power of God in this area to validate my freedom. Having tried several times to give up and failing almost instantly, I poured out my heart to Jesus that I wanted to be free. A short time after I came down the stairs one day, and I knew in my heart this was the day. I stopped smoking immediately and had no urge, no desire: I just completely stopped. I knew He had heard my prayer and had helped me.

Throughout my time at the rehab, we visited local churches to help us raise finance for the charity. It seemed so bizarre compared to my former life, unlike any experience I had ever had, but I loved to make Jesus known and longed for others to know Him in the same way. I knew if He set me free and healed me, He could do it for them. During these times of sharing my story, I found greater healing – every time I shared, I overcame a little more. I found as I asked God to use me to speak to those we visited, He would often lead me to emphasize different aspects of my journey, highlighting what Jesus had done. I needed to lean into Him as I was never sure how the words would come out, but each time it was as if Jesus had written the script word for word.

I had been in the home a year when I finally got the pass to go into a women's prison and share my story. I was so excited. My first visit was to HMP Newhall. Sue and Carla went with me. While we were waiting in the chapel to speak to the women, I was reminded that I did not need to pray to take Jesus with me, He was already there. I felt Him there, He was always there. I was reminded of times when He had steered me as a prisoner.

It was a real breakthrough moment where I gave hope to others, shared how my life had been transformed and impressed upon the women that if God could do it for me, He could do it for them. That was the beginning of many visits to both women's and men's prisons with women from Victory Outreach. It was sacred ground to me. We were on a 'rescue mission' to see as many as we could plucked out of slavery and hopelessness. These were great days of victory, that God could turn our lives around and use us to bring hope to others.

It is true to say that during my time in the rehab there were times when my buttons were really pressed my attitude could still stink. Yet, even in my frustrations and inner rebellion, I managed to comply with what was being asked of me on the programme. It was not always easy sticking to the programme, especially when things did not make sense to me.

I remember one day when I was furious with the constant demands and changes of our work programme, and my frustration with a staff member spilled out.

"I've had enough!" *What does she think I am?* As soon as the staff member turned her back to go indoors, I stormed off up the garden path.

My self-control has exceeded its limit and I threw down my tools. I was infuriated and I saw red: seeing no one around, I decided I had to get out of the house. You were not allowed to leave the rehab unescorted. Frustrated, I walked out of the gate with only the thought of getting away to get some space. I didn't want to run, so instead I went to the local shop and brought some cigarettes. I had not had a cigarette since quitting, but that day I had a very short-lived relapse in an attempt to relieve my frustrations. I hid behind a bin down an alley, smoking them back-to-back until I felt sick. It didn't solve anything; it just passed some time. I wandered along the road and, after a couple of hours, I was picked up by the staff who were out looking for me.

My eighteen months were drawing to a close, and that incident along with my restlessness meant that I was offered an opportunity at the rehab's smallholding with the directors. The new opportunities of helping to look after a horse and to get more involved with the prison work were incentives for me. The smallholding was also home to horses, donkeys, sheep, goats, a number of other animals and half a dozen female residents.

It was during my time at the smallholding that the Lord took me on a much-needed journey of learning to trust. The journey involved a horse called Sonny. I had met Sonny during my visits to the lodge, as those of us in the girls' home used to help on the animal project one day a week as part of our work programme.

Straight away, Sonny caught my eye – he reminded me of Black Beauty with his stunning glossy black coat. I was intrigued, as he always seemed to hang his head low. It reminded me of myself: my whole life I had walked with my head hung low in shame. Sonny never showed much interest in people, almost as though he would rather avoid them. When Lucy introduced me to him, she told me that his behaviour reminded her of a crackhead; he was unpredictable and sketchy. If you unnerved him, he would be likely to take a bite out of you! He had obviously learned this self-protective behaviour. Sonny was a rescue horse who had been badly treated and left to starve in a railway carriage. I felt like I understood his struggle and wanted the challenge to win his trust.

Now I was living over there, I was asked to take on this new responsibility for Sonny. It meant that I needed to commit, as I would not want to let him down, yet I wanted to be free to leave Victory Outreach whenever I chose to. It had never appealed to me to stay there long term like some did. I had been considering my next steps. I still lacked peace about the options I was considering. Alongside the offer to take care of Sonny, I was also offered an opportunity to become a training member of staff. I could not resist him or the opportunity to continue to grow, so I made the choice to take him on. Committing to looking after him was an interruption to my potential plans of moving on and a big step for me. I took any commitment seriously, which is why generally I avoided them.

Over time, I gained his trust and he gained mine. It took months for me to get close enough to have a nose rub, and for him to walk close by my side when I walked him over the fields. Sonny softened my heart and gave me someone I could truly love outside of Jesus, someone who would not hurt me, someone who I felt safe with and who would share my confidence. He was slowly teaching me to build and gain trust which gradually also helped bring me a step nearer to people.

While I was learning to trust, I had started to come out of my shell a little more. Rather than hiding in my room in my time off, I began to come out of hiding and mingle during the evenings as we sat down together in the lounge sharing on how the day had gone. I felt motivated to love others, supporting them in their journey by walking alongside them and sharing my faith and journey with them. I found great purpose in helping others to see the hope that is in Jesus. I had received so much. My heart overflowed with a desire to give back to others; God had saved me and His desire is that everyone would experience this love, joy, hope and freedom.

One of the things I learned about myself here was that I needed to be progressing or achieving to prevent boredom. I was not happy if I was stagnant; it was a dangerous place for me to be. Now I was now officially a training staff member, I had been given more responsibility for prison work: following up applications, writing letters, and being involved in visits. We would pray daily at eight thirty in the evening when we knew the prisoners were locked behind the door.

I stuck close to Dinah, who had begun the ministry, as I wanted to grow spiritually and learn everything I could from her. Dinah was petite, with blonde hair, and walked with a slight limp due to a bad hip. She was the first spiritual mother I had who reflected Jesus so evidently in many ways to me. I found her inspiring. She also had a fierce and passionate side, and she was nobody's fool.

I watched and learned much from her: how she handled the most challenging situations and how she ran the prison ministry. The more I went into the prisons, the more passionate I became about seeing women really freed from all that had imprisoned them, and I knew Jesus could do it. A few years down the line, I got into Eastwood Park, where I had been numerous times. Not being escorted through the gates, but walking in and back out as a free woman was quite a momentous moment for me. Seeing how far God had brought me only made me value Him and others more.

Whenever I stood in front of the women getting ready to speak, my stomach did somersaults, especially as it was always possible someone might be disruptive. They never were though, and if anyone tried, most of the other women would call them back into order. I was always so encouraged, honoured and delighted to tell the women that I had been in their position. I could tell them how I had lived and what I had been like, knowing that it resonated with them, and I knew some were shocked as they saw me as I was now. It was incredible: the moment I started to speak, they always showed the utmost respect, and there was such an unusual silence you'd be able to hear a pin drop in the room. I have to say, in all the places I have shared my story, prison has always been one of the most precious places – not because I feel at home but because His presence is always so strong.

Chapter 27: Forgiveness

One of the most significant realisations for me of the work of Jesus in my heart was coming face to face with a former sex offender. We had just been filming our testimonies at church. At a friend's house afterwards, I was sitting across a table from this guy, eating my fish and chips. I asked him his story, how he came to know Jesus. Having just heard my story, he looked at me and hesitated. There was a sombre silence, I could see the remorse in his eyes and still a glimmer of shame as he looked down and began to open up. He confessed he had been a child abuser until he met Jesus and that Jesus had changed his heart. He was quick to tell me how he had encountered the forgiveness of Jesus for his wrongs and how he was a new man in Christ, freed from that sickness. He seemed to recognise that although God had made him right with Him, because of his crimes, it would take society longer to accept Him. As I looked at him, I paused: I saw Jesus, I saw the cross, I felt the love of God well up in me and I knew that Christ had died not only for my sins but for his sins, too.

I recognised and believed that this man had a repentant heart, that he was sorry and genuinely receiving help and God was working on him. It was Christ in me in that moment that enabled me to see this man through His eyes. And this is the truth of the gospel: if we are truly sorry and turn away from our sins, God forgives us and renews us.

As I journeyed with God, I realised that forgiveness was also a big area in my life to work through. To be restored and fully free required me to forgive others and myself. Having been forgiven so much by Jesus, I found it easier to forgive others from that place. I learned that forgiveness was not saying that what happened did not matter. Rather, it was acknowledging the wrong but deciding to allow God to deal with other people's wrongs instead of holding onto it myself.

Over time, I was able to forgive those who had hurt me and let go of the wrongs done. I learned that holding onto unforgiveness caused resentment, that it was holding onto the pain attached to those events, enabling them to continue to impact my life negatively. Forgiving those who hurt me has been a gradual journey, one which Jesus has taken me on. It has resulted in being liberated from the pain attached to significant traumatic events that happened in my life.

I had to learn to forgive myself, to stop judging myself, condemning myself for my actions and for those things done to me. This has not been an easy journey, for I am my own worst critic, but I came to realise that if God forgave me, who was I to judge myself? There is no one greater than God and He chose not to condemn but to forgive me and set me free.

Two and a half years had passed, and I was still at the Lodge in Victory Outreach, but I was there as a free woman. I chose to stay after asking God to confirm if it was time to leave; I wanted to leave, but I had no peace and had been given an opportunity to go and do horse-riding at college. I had no experience, and it was not a place for commoners like me. I prayed and said to God, *I will get accepted into college if I am meant to stay.*

Five of us went for an assessment. Two of us were singled out to do some jumps. I had no experience, and I'm not sure how I made it through, but we were not offered a place, so I thought that was my sign not to stay. Within twenty-four hours, they contacted us and said they had changed their mind. I took this as my cue to stay a while longer. I learned that God is in the big miraculous moments in our lives but also in the little details that are important to us. When we engage with Him, things happen.

During the time I had been at Victory Outreach, I had been in contact with my sister, Marie, and then with my brother, Gary. Our relationships were gradually being restored as they maintained regular contact through visits and ongoing phone calls. This was the beginning of God reconnecting us. It was precious to me, as so many years had passed – in some ways I felt like I didn't know them anymore, and I was a completely different person. Their regular support saw me through my time at rehab and gave me confidence to eventually see the rest of the family, knowing I was strong enough and healed enough to see them. As a training staff member, I had been permitted a mobile phone and Eileen contacted me via my sister, as she had revealed to my family that she was in touch with me. I couldn't believe it when I heard her voice on the other end of the phone,

"How are you, Trudy?" she asked, in a slightly nervous tone. I didn't even ask how she had got my number; it was so comforting to hear her voice. It sounded so much more soothing now I was straight headed, and immediately I felt that connection with her. I told her about where I was – she loved animals and it made for good small talk – and she went on to tell me about her dog, how she had diabetes and how she was now in a wheelchair after losing her legs. My heart sank. She had been through so much, and regret welled up in me for not having been there.

"I want us to have a relationship," I said to her. "I am sorry for the pain and upset I caused, I hope that you can forgive me." There was a pause.

"Trudy, I love you and I am so happy that you are getting better. That's all I want – to see you happy."

Marie had given her my number as she was arranging for a family get together, and I had been permitted to go to my family for a couple of days. Prior to that, I had asked Marie not to let everyone know where I was, as I had messed up too many times. I was anxious about letting people down and about the emotions that may come up early on in my recovery, but now people would know and I would see the rest of them.

It was awkward seeing everyone after so long. Marie had even invited my old friend Saffron, who I had not seen in over ten years, to give me some moral support. Her being there helped me to escape the awkwardness of seeing everyone after so long.

"We missed you at Warren's funeral," Saffron said. "I kept looking around thinking you were going to walk through the door at any minute."

I had only just found out about Warren. He had taken an accidental drug overdose the first year I was in rehab, but my sister Marie had not told me for fear I would leave. It was really hard swallowing the fact that she had kept it from me for so long. I was gutted but chose to forgive her, knowing she just thought she was doing what was best.

"It was a good turnout, Trude. Loads of people came, you would have been pleased." I felt sad I had not been there, yet relief at the good turnout. The gang from back in the day were loyal and when we lost someone everyone turned out regardless. I wept; it was good to see her, but I knew I could not turn the clock back.

Soon after that I had become a full-time support worker. I had also started an NVQ Health and Social Care Level 3 to help me in my role as staff, along with the one day a week course for horse-riding. It was not long after that suddenly the girls' home fell into a bit of a crisis as they were without a manager. I was asked to stand in the gap and cover the home.

I spent a couple of months there helping out: sadly, the former managers had let the place go. I began redecorating and cleaning up the place, rebuilding the structure and support of the program for the residents to prepare to take more girls in. I was happy to stand in the gap and help out, but that was all – I didn't intend to become the manager on a full-time basis. However, during this time, Jesus really gave me a heart for the women and the work. It felt bizarre that I was managing the home after everything I had been unable to manage in my former life. I certainly couldn't see how I had been equipped for this. Then, one day Dinah really challenged me that I still avoided any decisions around commitment. Her provocations always seemed to have a positive outcome. It took a few weeks, but I came to a place where I found real peace and embraced this new opportunity wholeheartedly. I decided to take on the responsibility fully.

I spent the best part of the next five years as a live-in manager. It was a huge responsibility for me, running the home and leading three spiritual meetings a day. An almost immediate reverential fear of God developed within me as I sensed the weight and yet joy of this responsibility. I continued to manage the women's prison ministry from the home.

One afternoon I interviewed a young woman at HMP Eastwood Park, who had applied to come to Victory Outreach. As I sat opposite her, she pleaded with me to give her a chance, explaining how no one could help her. As the tears streamed down her face, I was so moved by her desire for help. She had accumulated so many labels and I knew on paper I should probably not take her. Seeking to reassure her, I said I would do my best to see if we could support her and remind her that we would have to speak to a number of key people in her case: police, probation, and someone from MAPPA, which deals with public protection. As I walked out of the prison that day, I cried out to God to use me to see those bound, tormented and held captive in their lives set free. She did come to us, and she received Jesus into her life and we saw incredible breakthroughs. She was one among so many that encountered the love of the Father, the forgiveness of a loving saviour and a home where she could belong and be loved.

In so many ways I felt unqualified to run the women's home, but knew I was called by God to do this work, and this helped me to lean more heavily on the Lord for His help in every minute of every day. One day, I sat in my office in the first few months of managing, feeling unsure about it all and dealing with feelings of unworthiness and inadequacy. Then suddenly, as clear as anything, I heard God's voice in my heart: *You are wired for this; everything up to now has prepared you.* I knew that without His help I wouldn't be able to journey with and help the women, deal with their emotions and guide them through their brokenness. Managing the home, the women, the daily programme, the house, money, the prison work, supporting the women, emotionally, spiritually and practically, along with everything else that came with it was the season that really shaped my dependence on Jesus. I truly saw Him carry, lead, help and sustain us all. It was one of the richest times of my life.

It truly became home for so many over those years. It was a place where the broken, the downtrodden and the marginalised came in with addictions, trauma and other life controlling issues. It was a home where these women found hope, healing and freedom. It was a place where lives were changed and transformed. These women discovered purpose and restoration for their lives through coming to know Jesus and His grace in their lives. It brought such a sense of richness and purpose to my own life, too.

Chapter 28: God's Plan

One Sunday, while I was manager, I met an Evangelist called Marilyn Harry. I had heard of her through one of the girls on the programme. She told me Marilyn ran a school of Evangelism called Harvest Time and how powerful the ministry of healing and deliverance was. One Sunday we attended Victory Outreach's newly established church and Marilyn was there. We said hello and she arranged to come and visit a girl she knew that was staying in the home.

Marilyn was glowing, warm, loving and friendly and her smile could put anyone at ease. After she had talked and prayed with the girl, we started chatting. She told me she was arranging a mission trip to India. My heart leaped: as a young girl I had heard the stories of Mother Theresa in India and always felt so much sympathy for those who were suffering there. I had dreamed of being able to go one day and help. Marilyn invited me to go to her home and have food with her and find out more about the trip. *It must be God at work*, I thought to myself. The truth was if there was anything I thought I would have been for the Lord, it would have been a mission partner: someone who goes to places to help local men, women and children practically and spiritually, and lead people to Jesus.

When I came home, I could not stop thinking about it. *Where on earth would I get the money?* My wage working for the charity was very small. I began to ask people to sponsor me to go, and they did. I was so sure this was God restoring His purposes for me. When Marilyn informed me that there had been unforeseen challenges that meant we were no longer able to go to India, I was devastated. She invited me to go to Rwanda in Africa instead. It had really been in my heart to go to India, and I was distressed: I had asked people to sponsor me for India.

I wrestled with Jesus over it, seeking Him. He confirmed three times that I should go. The first confirmation came through someone who was preaching and began to talk about Rwanda. The second was hearing about Rwanda on the news the same week. The third came at church: I asked Jesus to speak to me about Rwanda through the minister, but then one of the girls asked me to look at a book she was thinking of buying from their bookshop. I opened the book and there, on the top line, I read Rwanda. This was the Lord's confirmation. It was as if the Spirit was placing the word Rwanda on my agenda, and I made the decision to go.

During that first trip to Africa, I stood on the platform next to Marilyn and saw at least a couple of hundred people rush forward to receive Jesus Christ as their Saviour. It was one of the most significant moments of my life, and I knew that anything less than living this life would be unfulfilling. I also saw my first notable physical healing. A man who had been lame all his life came into one of our meetings; he came with a condition called hydrocephalus, which meant he had fluid on the brain that had caused him to suffer with paralysis all his life. We prayed for many to be healed that night and saw many healings. It was the next day, during a meeting, when this man came back with many from his village. He came to share how God touched and healed him. He came forward during the meeting. As he walked up the steps that led on to the stage, which was several feet high, beneath his arms he carried both his wooden crutches. Marilyn asked him what had happened.

"I was prayed for in the name of Jesus, and Jesus healed me!" he shouted.

With that, he threw his crutches away and leapt off the stage, landing on his feet and praising God, then ran round the building! The place erupted and that night, almost everyone responded to receive Jesus. That event left its mark on me. I had seen not only transformation and miracle in my life, through the women I worked with, but there in Africa I saw so many others receive Jesus and so many be healed. I knew my life would never be the same after this.

That was the beginning of many overseas trips for me. Since then, I've had the privilege of sharing, preaching, and teaching the word of God and raising funds to help poor communities in third world countries, in Europe and the UK. I also returned home with such a fresh vigour and desire to make Jesus known. I stayed connected with Marilyn, joining the Evangelism school on my days off, and I caught a passion for going out into the street, preaching and reaching communities with the transforming message of Jesus. It was something I found life-giving and it brought me great joy outside of the home.

During my ongoing time as the manager, I maintained contact with Eileen but couldn't see her much as my job took up all my time and attention. I only had a couple of years of contact with her before she then passed away in 2010. The pain of that loss was like nothing I could have prepared for. I knew the only other part of me in this world was gone; I felt such a sadness that she had gone so soon.

After Eileen passed away, I was reminded that I had been adopted into my family and that surely God must have had a purpose in mind. I decided that I would make every effort to build a relationship with my adopted parents. I had begun a forgiveness and healing journey in the first rehab but had a long way to go. However, I knew it was God's plan to use me to share Him with them. He loved them, He had forgiven me, and I knew His heart was for my family and for them to know this same love and forgiveness. I became intentional about visiting them several times a year and building bridges, then I invited them to visit. It was the first time in my five years of being clean that they had come to see me.

I saved up some money and put my parents up in a hotel; I'm not sure they had ever stayed in a hotel before. They visited the home and came to church with me. When we arrived at the church, it was heaving, packed to the brim: the presence of God was strong. That day, I was on the prayer team. I knew this environment was completely alien to them as they had only ever been in a Church of England service for weddings or christenings. When an appeal was given to those who wanted to say yes to receiving Jesus as their saviour, my dad responded! I watched him pray to receive Jesus.

"You know, I've always believed in God, Trudy," he was pleased to tell me over Sunday lunch that day. I was overjoyed and relieved all at the same time as he told me how he had come to believe.

I was even happier that he wanted to share this with me, but I was left wondering about my mum. So that night, in one last attempt to see her encounter God, I took them both to another church we had in Merthyr. I wondered if it was too much, but they were happy to come. As the minister spoke a message of hope and healing, we were sitting up high in the auditorium. My mum was on crutches at the time, and ill with all manner of things, so much so that you only had to look at her to see she was frail. The minister asked who wanted a healing touch from Jesus, and I was taken by surprise when my mum stood up of her own accord and began to walk down this steep set of stairs – it was not an easy manoeuvre. As I sat and watched her determination to go, something in me completely broke. Tears ran down my face as I saw her make her way down to the front to be prayed for. Warmth filled my heart and the residue of resentment I still had was washed away in a river of tears and compassion. I took them back that evening to the hotel and she looked so much lighter; I could see the visible difference and knew the Lord Jesus had touched her.

Two years later in 2013, the news came that I needed to get to the hospital as Mum was not going to make it. My mum was always complaining of having all manner of things wrong with her, but it was evident that this time, she was truly unwell. She had cancer.

I begged God to keep her till I got there. As I arrived, the family were all there. I sat by the side of my mother's bed; she looked so thin, scared, and kept saying she wanted to go home. I felt so sad that they would not permit her to leave the hospital. Knowing she had little time, I spoke with her again about Jesus and getting right with God. We prayed together for her to receive the Lord as her saviour.

"I am sorry, Trudy," she said, taking my hand in hers.

I welled up on the inside, unable to say anything. I wanted to tell her it was okay, but nothing came out.

In that moment, I felt that God had done inner heart surgery on me; something that day that had been lost was restored. Mum had made her peace with me and with God. The word of God tells us that He will restore the years that the locusts have eaten away, and I know this to be true. It was as though the pain had gone. I continued to sit with her, holding her hand and tending to her with a flannel as her temperature was up. In those moments I wanted her to feel loved and cared for. Within three days, she passed away.

A month after her passing, we had a move of God in the church that was started by the new director of Victory Outreach. The church had been going for a few years when, one night, a man came along who had been wheelchair bound for ten years. I knew him vaguely as someone who was attending the church. It was a night like any other: I encouraged the girls to go forward to receive prayer and walked with them to the front. Many people gathered, and the man in the wheelchair also came forward. We gathered round and our pastor began to pray. There was a sense of expectancy bubbling; God was moving. The pastor asked us all to pray over the man's legs as they began shaking, and then, suddenly he got out of the wheelchair, picked it up, lifted it over his head and ran around the room! The atmosphere was electric; everyone's eyes were on sticks! It was as though the heavens had opened and a light and glory so powerful descended upon that place, and for months after we saw people getting healed, saved and set free daily. The presence of God was so strong that people travelled from all over the world to come. I took the women to the meetings every night for months and saw their healing accelerated in the presence of God.

One night I was in bed and in my mind's eye I saw masses of people in a stadium responding to the call to follow Jesus. I was amazed and I felt the Lord whisper to my heart, *'Why not you?'* This picture was like a vision, a window of invitation into the future. What I saw was impossible to achieve in the natural sense for me, but I know anything is possible with God when you believe what He says and shows you.

As I saw the vision, I was overwhelmed at the change in me as a result of meeting Jesus. Where once my voice seemed to be stolen, shut down and silenced, God had restored it and was demonstrating to me that He was going to use my voice to bring others to see His love and power at work in them.

Another evening, I attended a meeting in Kensington Temple London with Victory Outreach, when a woman sought me out.

"God is going to use you and your story to preach the Good News of Jesus," she told me. "Don't be afraid to use your story to preach from."

While I was there, I picked up a copy of The Revival Times magazine and brought it home. After everyone had gone to bed, I picked up the magazine and flicked through. I saw an advert for a Bible College at Kensington Temple. It was like it leapt out of the pages at me.

No way! I thought. I closed the magazine tight and threw it down on the floor. I believed it was the Spirit of God prompting me. Several days later, I was still bothered at my response and disobedience to the promptings of the Spirit. I looked again through the magazine but couldn't find the advert. I wondered if it was my imagination playing tricks on me.

Later that week, I went to visit my good friend Marilyn Harry who was organising a mission trip to France.

"We will be staying with good church friends in France," she told me when I arrived. "Also, the Bible College in France, which is part of Kensington Temple in London, will be with us."

That got my attention: *Kensington Temple Bible College*. I decided to pay close attention to what God may be saying while we were there; it was a time to seek Him for the next steps.

Chapter 29: Moving On

After seven years of being in Victory Outreach, I felt restless. I knew that the Lord was preparing me to move on. In 2013 I moved out into a bedsit nearby, travelling in for work. This was part of God gently drawing me away. Victory Outreach was all I had known for seven years, first living and then working there. So many transformative things had happened during my time at the home. I have so many incredible memories of walking with the wounded and broken, loving them back to life, introducing them to Jesus and teaching them a new way of living.

I had felt the tenderness of God beginning to almost unstitch me from Victory Outreach, as though He was gently removing me, and I was reminded how God always handles us with great care. I began to seek Him for the future. With this in mind, I had done what I could to prepare others to take over from me as the manager so that transition would go well. Up to this point, I had not been sure of what was next. I had considered going to China as a missionary and had begun learning Chinese. From the time I came to the Lord, I always knew preaching, missions and sharing my faith were key to what God had in mind for me.

The week we were in France, I sought God for my next steps. While we were there, we saw many people give their life to Jesus, wonderful healing and people being set free. During one service, when God moved so powerfully, I found myself under the power of God curled up in a foetal position on the floor. I wept and wept: God was doing a deep inner work. After that service, as we ate our food, I saw a father holding a baby close to his chest and I felt the Lord whisper, *That's how you will always be to me, no matter what age you are.*

During our time in France, I was also reminded of a vision I had of the stadium. I remember hardly daring to believe and I heard his whisper again, '*Why not you?*' I kept this in my heart, continuing to seek him for the next steps.

When I came back, I knew I wanted to pursue this idea. I looked up Regents Theological Bible College, an Elim church college, as I knew a friend who had been there. The pictures looked too grand for me. *I just won't fit in.* Put me in the mess of life and I would do well, yet I was not sure I was good enough for a place like this. I still struggled a bit with a feeling of inferiority. I never told anyone I was looking!

I decided to pursue an application for Kensington Temple Bible College as well, just to be sure that wasn't where God wanted me instead. As I was attending a 'Just Looking' day at Regents, I struggled with doubts: I was part of a move of God in my church, I was also living with miracles day in day out, so was I sure this was right?

On my way back, I went to our nightly revival meeting at the church that had been going on for a couple of months now. My pastor approached me.

"Trudy, have you thought about Bible College?" *How did he know?*

"Well, actually," I said, "I have been thinking about it. I have been considering Kensington Temple Bible College."

"The Elim college would be a much better place for you to go, you'll get the best there. I'd happily give you a reference."

This was a change of tune: when I had asked him about doing the school of Evangelism, I knew he was against it for fear of me leaving, but he could now see I was ready to fly the nest. His words helped in the final decision to apply. So, I applied to the Elim Regents Bible College, and then a bit later to Kensington Temple.

I ended up getting accepted into Regents College, which I thought frankly was too upmarket for me, but God had made a way. In the selection process, I was asked to write a short essay about the very message I had been preaching at that time in local churches. Knowing that my grammar and English were hindered due to skiving school, I wondered whether I could possibly be accepted to do a degree, but I was!

As time to leave for college drew closer, I felt God whisper to me, *"I am going to give you one thousand pounds."* I questioned myself: was I sure that was Him speaking?

The following Sunday, as I drove the girl's bus to church, I felt the Lord instruct me to put all the money I had into the offering. That was a big ask. I had two hundred pounds, which was a huge amount to me in those days.

"Ok, Lord," I thought. *"Can I put one hundred in now and one hundred in later?"* I needed to get my head around it. I didn't hear anything else, but I decided to do it. When I got to church, before I even put the money in the offering basket, my pastor approached me.

"The Lord has told me to give you a thousand pounds."

I couldn't believe it! I have never ceased to be astounded at how the Lord provides. Of course, I put the extra hundred in with joy!

That May, I suddenly received a call.

"Dad died in his sleep!" my sister wept on the phone.

"I'm coming!" I cried, still in shock. "Please don't let them take Dad till I get there and see him."

I could not believe this was happening. I felt I had just got my dad back, and now he was gone. As I arrived at the house, everyone was in shock. I walked into the bedroom where my sister had found him. I lay on the bed next to him and held him, knowing I would never see him again after this moment. I stayed as long as I could, grateful to have the moment. My heart was truly broken. He was a huge loss, one that was more difficult for me to work through.

The time soon came. 2013 was a big year: I lost both my parents, I had moved out of Victory Outreach into my own place, and I had left all I had known, my stability and security of the last seven and a half years. It was the presence of Jesus that saw me though.

While I was at Bible College, I would pray and ask God about my next steps. I gradually had an increasing sense that God wanted me to share His word and the good news with others so that they could encounter Him like I had and experience His presence and power at work in their lives. God took what was broken and stolen in my life and restored it; He then chose to use my voice and story as another means to show others that He truly does heal and restore our lives when we follow Him.

It was only in my second year at college that I really felt joy begin to come back into my life. The first year had been great but, in my grief, I felt unable to really consider the future; I just took one day at a time. While others talked of ministry and becoming an Elim Minister in Training, I never had that passion. However, during that second year, as I studied the history of the Elim movement, my spirit began to leap again. I was inspired and invigorated with a fresh hunger to see God move in our nation. Elim had a history of seeing salvation, healing and miracles that I longed to see more of.

The college dean talked to me about applying to become an Elim Minister in Training. I still wasn't sure if I should definitely stay with the Elim movement, yet it seemed that God was moving me in this direction. I went with it and, to my surprise, I was accepted. After visiting, I had an offer for the future to be a part of the church team. I had no idea what that would look like, but it was a requirement that a Minster in Training, or MIT, serve in a local church until ordained. It was amazing that this opportunity opened up for me – it was in Bristol, where I had lived for years as an addict on the streets and where God had taken me back, this time as a light and a sign of God's power to others.

When I first started my MIT in Bristol, myself and Jake made contact. We agreed to meet up. I was apprehensive but wanted a chance to say sorry. I knew when I had last seen him, he had harboured a lot of resentment and blame towards me. I hoped it could finally be put right. I felt in some ways responsible, and it burdened me, so I wanted to have that opportunity. I pulled up on the road to meet him, he jumped in the car, and we pulled away.

"Nice, you have your own car now!" he said, checking out my little Fiat. The last time we had a run-around, it was short lived and none of us were legal. He looked thin, worn in the face. His beautiful smile had deteriorated. I smiled as if not to make a big deal.

"It's really good to see you, Jake. I'm glad to know you're okay. Over the years I have often wondered how you are doing."

"I live here," he said, indicating out of the window. "I just want to get changed." I pulled up and he invited me in.

The place was rented, it was a mess, but I had seen worse. He told me he was doing fine and he was clean, but what he meant was he was not as bad as he had been. It was obvious to me he was on a slippery slope. He went upstairs to get changed and I paced around downstairs waiting for him. When he came back down, I knew he'd gone to use, too. He started to talk about how things were for him, and I listened patiently. I was waiting to share with him how my life had changed so much after meeting Jesus, that he had changed my heart and transformed my life.

"Jake, I'm sorry for the way I was. I hope you're able to forgive me."

He brushed it off and started to say he'd moved on and what he'd been up to over the years. I could see he was still waiting for me to slip back into the old me. I took him to the lake to sit outside and have a drink, eager to listen to him and to have an opportunity to continue to share with him. He got a pint.

"What, you don't want a drink or a smoke?" he asked.

"I don't do it anymore, Jake. I am happy without them, I don't need them." He was shocked and looked at me with a serious stare. As we spent time together, it was sinking in for him that things were different. I told him that the Lord wanted to restore him, but he said he was not ready for that yet. After a while, we strolled back to the car.

"You really have changed, Trudy," he said.

I knew he was intrigued by all I had told him and all that he saw. I left him, praying that one day he would also find the freedom I have found.

Through my time at college, I had asked God to confirm again that He wanted me to share the good news. I was unsure, as I couldn't quite believe He really was saying it to me. It was while on placement that I was asked to preach a short message at a baptism service. I asked God that morning for at least one person to give their life to Jesus — as I concluded my message, I saw thirteen people come forward to receive Jesus!

I completed my course in June 2016 with a Bachelor of Arts 2:1 in Applied Theology and Church Leadership. This was a miracle; I recollected how desperately I prayed to God in my first year to pass and get through. It was a huge step for me at forty years old, one I had never dreamt possible. As I received my results, I was overwhelmed with emotion at the accomplishment I had worked so hard for. I had loved every minute: the learning, the stretching, and the three-year journey with wonderful friends. It seemed surreal it was coming to the end. During our final, commissioning day I was awarded the George Jefferies award for Evangelism, which was another significant sign of God's encouragement towards His purposes for me. George Jefferies was the pioneer Evangelist of Elim Pentecostal churches, which saw the movement born and multitudes come to faith and get healed. His story had been my biggest inspiration at college. It was a wonderful day, Marilyn and Simon were there, those people that I had considered so important in this journey.

Epilogue: Nothing Wasted

During my time ministering in Bristol, God has done many wonderful things. I have had so many opportunities to share this message of hope with people. I've been able to share with those I have known and used with, those caught in addiction and hopelessness, with the homeless and broken. Whilst God will use our life experiences, they do not need to define us. He has always put me in places where I can help all kinds of people from diverse backgrounds different to mine which I find astounding.

Being back in Bristol helped me to see just how much I had changed. As I rode the streets looking for girls to speak to, it seemed another world away from who I had become. It was amazing what God had done in setting me free from drugs. Sometimes I would have flashbacks, but I was no longer the girl who had no value for herself and deemed herself unworthy of love or who ran to escape her pain. Instead, I took care of myself, knowing that God loved me and my value came from Him, not from others' treatment or perception of me.

During my years of training, there were times I experienced new levels of insecurity around male authority. Being in this new context around male leadership, I recognised I still behaved in ways to keep myself safe. God was revealing a root of rejection and abandonment that had come in as a child and been compounded; my self-protective behaviours were based around shame, fear and rejection. I learned that while I had changed the way I thought, I still had some old coping mechanisms from childhood.

The fear of rejection told me if people really knew me, they would not want me. God wanted to take me deeper into His love, which drives out all fear. Knowing how much God loves me enables me to feel safe when difficult thoughts and feelings come up. I don't need to run away, but to run to Him. He counsels, heals and helps transform my wrong thinking and the behaviours that limit the life He intends for me. I have grown so much. It has sometimes been joyful, sometimes very challenging. Throughout, it has been the most wonderful thing to know that He is perfecting His work in me.

In 2020, God miraculously made a way for me to buy my own home. When I arrived in Bristol, God provided a home through a wonderful couple who I have come to love dearly as my own family. Staying with them for three years enabled me to save. I had been sensing I needed to take more responsibility and that God wanted to give me the longing of my heart for my own home. With a small deposit, I stepped out in faith to look in Wales, as I could not afford Bristol. One day, I visited a home that exceeded what I could afford. I loved it as soon as I arrived and, visiting other properties, I felt God whisper to me about this one. The day before I was due to visit the broker and estate agent, I was given a wonderful gift of three thousand pounds. This meant I now had a deposit of £10,000. I was able to put in an offer of £110,000 that day, which they accepted!

As someone who had spent so many years homeless, living on the street and moving around, this was almost unbelievable to me, and once again a sign of God's power, provision and promise in my life. Although I had come home to the Lord, I still lacked a physical home where I could finally rest from wandering from place to place. For me it is significant to have a base I can travel from, and know I have a pillow to snuggle into when I arrive home. It also showed me just how much the Lord cares about us and how He never misses a detail in our lives. It seems with God, there are no limits to what He can do with a life surrendered to Him.

That year continued to bring breakthrough: in the October, after four and a half years of training, I was ordained officially as an Elim minister.

My closest friend Marilyn came to my house, and we sat in the front room of my home, anticipating the moment.

"I'm so pleased to be with you on such a special day!" Marilyn said, as we sat before a screen ready to tune in. Due to the pandemic, the ordination of ministers was going to be happening over Zoom. I was grateful to have my greatest encourager with me, someone I am honoured to call a friend and spiritual mother, someone so full of compassion and faith. She is my closest confidant, an example of a dynamic woman of faith and a true inspiration. As I sat there, I became acutely aware of the magnitude of this breakthrough, how significant this moment was in the sight of God.

As I came to say my vows before God with everyone else on screen, I experienced the presence and power of God and was overcome with emotion. It had been a long road – a challenging, testing and refining road – and in that moment, I felt God's presence profoundly in the room. Having had to learn, train and grow in my ministry over four and a half years, I sensed His affirmation and approval in this moment. Marilyn then laid hands on me and prayed for me: this was marvellous in my eyes. Who would have considered that someone from my background could possibly become someone that God would choose in this way to serve Him and others?

Coming to the end of writing this book, I can't help but reflect on how different my daily life looks these days. It is so far removed from those I lived fifteen years ago. Let me give you a taste of a recent Friday.

In the morning, I served at our community outreach project, Street Church, where we welcome the homeless, addicts and the vulnerable, offering spiritual and practical support, prayer, signposting and befriending. It was a busy morning, and I was soon called over to help one of the women.

"Pastor Trudy, can you come and speak to Claire?"

Claire, a traumatised alcoholic, was sitting slumped over with an empty stare, tears filling her eyes. I sat and listened as she rambled and cried. It was the first time she allowed me to get close and pray. I was able to listen and wrap my arms around her as she wept. As I spoke words of life and hope over her, I felt God break in and calm her, giving her some peace and release her from the torment.

It was a good morning, as I was also able to pray with several other people. One man gave his life to Jesus, as God had clearly been drawing him closer. Another guy, who has a notorious reputation had just come out of jail, allowed me to pray for him. As I laid hands on him and prayed, he broke down, saying it was the first time in years he had felt any emotion. Another man who had been struggling to walk was stunned as I prayed for the pain to go in the name of Jesus.

"I can't believe it's gone!" he cried. Another guy's headache completely left him as we prayed. It was smiles all round!

"You know Jesus loves you and cares about all areas of your life," I told him.

When we were finished, I headed over to the office to prepare for launching our new food bank. I thanked God for being with me. The afternoon was busy as usual with work. I made several calls and started to prepare a message I wanted to share on the streets Sunday afternoon. Next, I had an appointment with a lady who really needed freedom from bitterness. That day I was able to see her receive that freedom; God touched her life as she chose to forgive, and immediately her face changed as she experienced a great release.

Finally, I visited one of our elderly congregation members, who is a widow. Although I am her pastor, I am aware that God places us in families and the church is a beautiful expression of God's family where all are welcome. I had gone to uplift and encourage her, but I also came away encouraged and richer for the visit.

That evening, I went to visit some friends and have some food together. We sat around chatting, eating, laughing, and discussing one of our favourite topics – how we love to dance! We went on to share and dreams and hopes for the future. Mine overflowed out of me.

"I want to travel the nations with the Gospel, run festivals of hope for communities, write books, see the sick healed, and see people set free, falling in love with Jesus and finding abundant life!"

I was tired, but as we continued inspiring and encouraging one another to live our best life, I carried a deep contentment knowing God is with me. I left that evening to head home to Wales feeling blessed and still in awe of what God had done so far, knowing the greatest adventures still lie before me.

> *"And we know that God causes everything to work together for the good of those who love God and are called according to his purpose for them."* (Romans 8:28 NLT)

God has turned my mess into a message of hope. The journey to Him has not been easy, and God never intended for me to go through so much heartache and pain. I have come to learn that we live in a broken world full of broken people, and damaged people break things – but when we truly trust in Him, God restores and heals anything that has been broken. It was only in receiving God's gift of salvation through Jesus that things began to really change for me. I was changed internally, and that changed my life externally, which is why it looks so different today. I have travelled to different parts of the world and seen Him do so many incredible works and miracles, both in me and the lives of others.

My journey with Jesus has been the greatest adventure of my life; I cannot imagine my life any other way now. The journey has been full of wonderful moments of coming to life, healing, freedom, experiencing love, peace, hope, joy and many miraculous occurrences of which there are too many to possibly capture in this one book.

Since I came to know Jesus, my heart and passion has always been to make Him known to anyone and everyone. However, I have always been particularly drawn to the most downtrodden and broken, perhaps because of my own story. I have seen the evidence and power of the word of God worked out in my own life. If He can do it for me and countless others, He can do it for you. There is no one beyond the reach of His mercy, love, forgiveness and healing.

God can take everything you give Him and turn it around for good. He is a miracle-working God. Nothing is beyond Him; nothing is too difficult for Him. My life is evidence of the fact that God will take the good, the bad and the ugly, and if you trust Him, He will make something beautiful out of it all. As we allow God to work in us and heal us, He takes our brokenness and turns it into a blessing by using those things in our lives to bless and help others.

> *"He comforts us in all our troubles so that we can comfort others. When they are troubled, we will be able to give them the same comfort God has given us."* (2 Corinthians 1:4 NLT)

I am excited by the uncertainty of what lies ahead, because I know that the One who holds the future is the same One who holds me in the palm of His hands. I am forever His, and I choose to live and remain in His love because He is a good father, a wonderful friend, a mighty God, and a loving saviour.

For several years I had known in my heart that God had wanted me to write a book, but I never considered my story was worthy, and I had put it off as life became busy. Yet I believe God spoke clearly to my heart during the early months of the pandemic and said, '*It's time for the book, it's time to write your story.*' As I come to the end of this chapter, I know my story is still being written.

Yours is, too. The question is, will you trust Him with your story?

Today you can begin by taking the first step by inviting Jesus into your life and allow your story to become part of His story for your life just like I did by praying the prayer below:

Heavenly Father,

I thank you for demonstrating your love for me by sending Jesus, your one and only Son, to die on the cross for me. Thank you that He died and rose again so I may have access to this new life and know forgiveness and peace with you. I ask you to forgive me for the wrong things I have done in my life. Fill me with the Holy Spirit as I trust you with my life and story.

Amen

Acknowledgements

I would like to thank my editor, Ali, for helping me bring the final manuscript together, for her support, dedication and commitment to me and the book. Getting to know you has been a joy and your handling of my work has been something I will forever be grateful for; you were the right person for me. I would also like to thank my friend Sal, for reading through my very first draft and helping with some editing and inputting into it in the early days. I want to thank Barry Woodard for his endorsement of the book. Your friendship, encouragement, support, and wisdom has been key in this journey. I am forever grateful to you. I want to thank Marilyn for always believing in me, for supporting me and being a voice of love and wisdom in my life, and for her support in my decisions for the book. Thank you to my pastor and colleague, Steve McEwen, his wife Anouscha, and my church family for their encouragement as I have gone on in this journey, and for their support in helping to publish the book. Thank you especially to Malcolm Down and Sarah Grace Publishing for believing in me and enabling me to publish my story.

I want to thank Emma for her friendship, recognise her incredible gift as an artist, thank you for your contribution to the cover of the book.

I want to acknowledge and thank those who have been a part of my journey along the way in every season of life; my life has become richer for the memories and experiences I have had.

I want to acknowledge those I have loved and lost along the way: Mum, Dad, Eileen, Grandad, Warren, Andy, Mel, Dean, Billy. Whilst life was not always easy, I want to say thank you for being a part of my story.

Organisations and Charities

Mind: mental health, addiction, suicide, self-harm, eating disorders
Call – 0300 123 3393
Web – https://www.mind.org.uk/information-support/helplines
Email – info@mind.org.uk
Text – SHOUT to 85258

Teen Challenge UK: rehab
Call – Willoughby House: 01664 822 221, Hope House: 01269 844 114
Web – http://www.teenchallenge.org.uk/about
Email – admissions@teenchallenge.org.uk

Hope Centre Cwmbran: rehab
Call - 01495 757 517
Web - http://www.hopecm.co.uk

Victory Homes Manchester: rehab
Call - 0161 737 6624
Web - https://www.vomanchester.org.uk
Email - info@vomanchester.org.uk

Refuge: domestic violence
Call - 0808 2000 247
Web: https://www.nationaldahelpline.org.uk

Rape Crisis: rape
Call - 0808 802 9999
Web - https://www.rapecrisis.org.uk

SupportLine: rape, suicide, self-harm

Call – 01708 765 200

Web – https://www.supportline.org.uk/contact-us

Email – info@supportline.org.uk

Rethink: suicide, self-harm

Call – 0808 801 0525

Web – https://www.rethink.org

Unseen: modern slavery

Call – 08000 121 700

Web – https://www.unseenuk.org

Beloved: sex industry

Call – 07541 366 577

Web – https://www.beloved.org.uk

Email – hello@beloved.org.uk

Beyond The Streets: sex industry

Call – 0800 133 7870

Web – https://www.beyondthestreets.org.uk

Email – support@beyondthestreets.org.uk

Samaritans

Call – 116 123

Web – https://www.samaritans.org/

Email – jo@samaritans.org

Contact

To contact Trudy, please email her at the address below:

info@trudymakepeace.com

Or write to her at E5 Bristol, 3-15 Jamaica Street, Bristol, BS2 8JP

Also available from Trudy: 'Ministering to Addicts' - a free downloadable resource for Evangelists and church leaders.